MAY THE (LORD BLESS)
YOU !!

- HENRY

PRAISE FOR
FAITH DRIVEN ENTREPRENEUR

As an entrepreneur who feels deeply called to the market-place, I am grateful for the experience and wisdom shared in this book around generosity, identity, and the unique challenges and opportunities of using business as a way to bring justice, equality, mercy, and dignity to earth as it is in heaven.

LIZ FORKIN BOHANNON
Cofounder and CEO of Sseko Designs and author of *Beginner's Pluck: Build Your Life of Purpose and Impact Now*

I was very sincere in my intent to create a faith-driven company—but the outcome was lukewarm at best. I know had I read *Faith Driven Entrepreneur* I would have, with new knowledge, fully accomplished my vision. This is a must-read for the believing entrepreneur!

HORST SCHULZE
Former president of the Ritz-Carlton

Christians know that their work is a part of their worship. But the how hasn't always been as clear. *Faith Driven Entrepreneur* will give you practical, actionable ways to build on your faith and integrate it into how you lead, launch, and grow your business.

SANYIN SIANG
Leadership coach, executive director of the Coach K Center on Leadership & Ethics at Duke University, and author of *The Launch Book*

Faith-driven entrepreneurship is an ancient-future proposition. From the time Abraham, Isaac, and Jacob lived as entrepreneurs on a faith adventure up to the present era, it has been a historical norm for God to work with people in the midst of the marketplace. Our world is groaning for the gospel, and business leaders following Jesus are poised for radical impact. This book needs to be read by every Christian businessperson, student, investor, and pastor. Let's go!

MIKE SHARROW
CEO of C12 Group

The top can be a lonely place, but *Faith Driven Entrepreneur* is a reminder that there are cofounders and CEOs all around the world working to faithfully serve God in the way they lead their businesses. I'm striving to be one of those leaders, and I invite anyone who reads this book to join me.

ANTHONY TAN
CEO of Grab

There are so many entrepreneurs in the world who haven't yet experienced the joy, freedom, and missional possibility of deeply connecting their work to their faith. Henry has pursued and lived out this integrated life and is now on a mission with J. D. and Chip to help thousands more through this book. Read it and you will no doubt be encouraged in your own journey.

DAVE BLANCHARD
Cofounder and CEO of Praxis

In 2008 in Charlotte, North Carolina, I felt very alone and very unsure of how to start a bank that sought to love God and love people. In *Faith Driven Entrepreneur*, Henry, J. D., and Chip do a wonderful job describing how God is moving around the globe. Entrepreneurship is the key to unleashing the next generation of Christ followers who are seeking to love God and love people. In this book, you'll find out why and how. My only complaint is that it was not available to guide me on my journey a decade ago!

CASEY CRAWFORD
CEO of Movement Mortgage

If you feel that starting a business can't be a part of God's plan for your life, think again. *Faith Driven Entrepreneur* is a book by entrepreneurs for entrepreneurs that invites all business owners—from the billion-dollar company to the street-corner store—to be a part of God's witness on earth.

DR. BRIAN FIKKERT
Founder and president of the Chalmers Center at Covenant College and coauthor of *When Helping Hurts: How to Alleviate Poverty without Hurting the Poor . . . and Yourself*

FAITH DRIVEN ENTREPRENEUR

Henry Kaestner, J. D. Greear,
and Chip Ingram

FAITH

DRI>EN

Entrepreneur

What It Takes to <u>Step Into Your Purpose</u>
and <u>Pursue Your God-Given Call</u> to Create

TYNDALE
MOMENTUM®

The Tyndale nonfiction imprint

Visit Tyndale online at tyndale.com.

Visit Tyndale Momentum online at tyndalemomentum.com.

Tyndale, Tyndale's quill logo, *Tyndale Momentum*, and the Tyndale Momentum logo are registered trademarks of Tyndale House Ministries. Tyndale Momentum is the nonfiction imprint of Tyndale House Publishers, Carol Stream, Illinois.

Faith Driven Entrepreneur: What It Takes to Step Into Your Purpose and Pursue Your God-Given Call to Create

Cover designed by Faceout Studios, Spencer Fuller

Interior designed by Dean H. Renninger

Edited by Jonathan Schindler

For information about special discounts for bulk purchases, please contact Tyndale House Publishers at csresponse@tyndale.com, or call 1-855-277-9400.

Library of Congress Cataloging-in-Publication Data

A catalog record for this book is available from the Library of Congress.

ISBN 978-1-4964-5723-3

Printed in the United States of America

27	26	25	24	23	22	21
7	6	5	4	3	2	1

CONTENTS

Foreword by Lecrae xi

Introduction (Henry Kaestner) 1

CHAPTER 1 Our Call to Create (Henry Kaestner) *5*

CHAPTER 2 Identity in Christ (Henry Kaestner) *15*

CHAPTER 3 Stewardship vs. Ownership (Chip Ingram) *25*

CHAPTER 4 In Partnership (Henry Kaestner) *41*

CHAPTER 5 Don't Worship Work (J. D. Greear) *51*

CHAPTER 6 Faith, Family, Work, and Fitness (Henry Kaestner) *67*

CHAPTER 7 Excellence Matters (Henry Kaestner) *81*

CHAPTER 8 Faithful vs. Willful (Chip Ingram) *89*

CHAPTER 9 Ministry in Deed (Henry Kaestner) *105*

CHAPTER 10 Ministry in Word (Henry Kaestner) *115*

CHAPTER 11 From Everywhere to Everywhere
(J. D. Greear) *125*

AFTERWORD Entrepreneurs and Pastors Need Each Other
(Chip Ingram) *135*

Acknowledgments 147

Discussion Guide 151

Notes 161

About the Authors 163

FOREWORD

What does it mean to be a Faith Driven Entrepreneur?

What does it mean to be a Faith Driven person . . . really?

These are questions I find myself asking often. This book has helped me move toward answers.

It's written for Christian entrepreneurs, yes, but there's something about that phrase—*Faith Driven*—that makes me think.

Christian makes a phenomenal noun but a subpar adjective. Because when you say "I am a Christian," you're saying a lot about who you are, right? You're saying that you stand for Jesus and that you're a follower of his. So often, though, that word *Christian* has a loose meaning.

If I told you I was a "Christian" plumber, what exactly does that mean? I'd like to imagine that a Christian plumber is someone you instantly knew operated with quality, excellence, integrity, timeliness, and many other virtues. That would be awesome if whatever came after the adjective *Christian* meant that. But oftentimes it doesn't.

This book is helping us redefine the idea of excellence by giving us a different frame. We're *Faith Driven*.

What does that mean? First and foremost, it says that my faith in Jesus Christ drives the way I work and live. It says that I'm here to create quality work. It says that I'm here to do the work that God has put in my hands to the best of my ability because I believe that he oversees everything I do, and my work, my time, my energy—all things that belong to and come from him—are tools to serve him well.

It's so easy to take those things and use them to glorify ourselves, though. Oftentimes we find ourselves fighting to keep up the image, fighting to keep up the persona of all the things that a Christian leader is "supposed" to be. And what ends up happening is that there's too much shame to be vulnerable and transparent about the areas where we are not succeeding and not winning because there are so many expectations on us.

When you're performing for acceptance, that's religiosity to the core. That's not faith.

Faith is when you can be honest and transparent and say, "God, I don't have what it takes. I need you to do it." I've chronicled my own journey of coming to the conclusion that I was more devoted to my devotion to God than I was devoted to his devotion to me. It's easy to get that backward, especially as an entrepreneur when you're the one who is constantly on the pedestal. You're the one everyone is looking at.

For Christians, we can be tempted to twist our virtues so

that they serve us. We like to pat ourselves on the back and say, "Look at me. I woke up at 5:00 a.m. to drink coffee and do my Bible study." Click. Instagram that. #blessed. But then people can look at us and think we're always the 5:00 a.m. Bible study and coffee type. We're not allowed to struggle. We're not allowed to fail. Entrepreneurs feel that pressure more than most, but the principles in this book can help relieve us of that burden. Why? Because it's not about us anyway.

I'm excited for the work that Henry, J. D., and Chip put into this book because of what it means to me as both an entrepreneur and a creator. They help us expand the definition of *entrepreneur* to include artists, musicians, builders, and anyone else who is making something new. Anyone who is following the example of their Creator God can find echoes of their work in this book.

I'm reminded that creativity is really a unique aspect of expressing what theologians would call "imago Dei"—the truth that we have been made in the image of God. God is the ultimate Creator, so he is the source of all creativity. He created the heavens, the earth, the moon, and the stars. And so when we are creating, we're actually reflecting his glory. We're reflecting back the awesomeness that he has instilled in us.

Paul tells us that "we are God's handiwork, created in Christ Jesus to do good works, which God prepared in advance for us to do" (Ephesians 2:10). And so, when I create, I know that in some sense I'm walking in God's footsteps. But the other beauty of creating is that it reminds me of how big God is.

God created something out of nothing. We can't even begin to imagine how that works. Instead, we use the raw materials that God has created to make things as our way of following his example. But one cool thing that we get to do that no other creature on the planet can do is add value to things. We can take ore and metal and then shape them and mold them, and then we add value to them in the same way God took dirt and added value to it by breathing life into it.

That's something really special that I don't want to take for granted. When people hear a song that I've made and they see it as valuable enough to want to purchase it, that's me following in the footsteps of God. I've just taken sounds and thoughts and added value to them—turning raw materials into something more. If you're an entrepreneur, you know the feeling.

Creating something that others want feels incredible. The only thing that tops it is creating something that makes others want something bigger than you could ever make. I believe the future is full of Faith Driven Entrepreneurs who will do just that—men and women around the world working to create products and services that meet the needs of those around them and point to the God who meets *all* our needs.

I hope I get to be one of those people. I hope you do too.

Lecrae

INTRODUCTION

Henry Kaestner

Blank stares.

That's what we saw in meeting after meeting, conference room after conference room. As we made the rounds up and down Sand Hill Road, we walked in and out of venture capitalists' offices, trying to figure out what had gone wrong. There were meetings where the disconnect was obvious. Many investors failed to resonate with different aspects of our business. But even for those who were interested in what we were doing, the mood changed when we talked about our faith. When we introduced that topic, there seemed to be a tension and unease that hadn't been there before.

I don't think this is a rarity for Faith Driven Entrepreneurs—the men and women who are starting companies and building businesses with a belief in Jesus Christ and an understanding of themselves as beloved children of God as their core identity.

In fact, I think many Christian entrepreneurs have received this response, either in a pitch meeting or even in their church.

Just as many venture capitalists are confused by how faith can be integrated into entrepreneurship, so too are many pastors and churchgoers. Many of us have misunderstood how entrepreneurs are core to the work God is doing on earth. Entrepreneurs aren't God's plan B. Rather, they are the men and women God has called and equipped to see his will done on earth as it is in heaven.

As an entrepreneur, you—yes, *you*—are a part of God's plan A. God has a purpose and a plan for the entrepreneurial ventures his people are starting and growing all around the world. The work you do today—the company you've built, the employees you work with, the customers you serve, the shareholders you report to, all of it—can serve as an active part of what God is doing on earth.

Faith Driven Entrepreneur is both an organization and a type of person. As an organization, we exist to encourage, equip, and empower Christ-following, entrepreneurially minded people with world-class content and community. As people, we (and hopefully you) are working to create, alongside the master Creator, businesses and enterprises that bring him glory through their mission, their return, and their practices.

But more than that, Faith Driven Entrepreneur is a movement. It is a continually growing group of people who believe that they are sent by God to do his work by building businesses that serve his plan.

Entrepreneurship is a lonely journey. But it doesn't have to be. You don't have to build your business on an island. Let this be an affirmation and a call to arms—your work matters, and you're not the only one out there doing it!

There are 582 million entrepreneurs in the world—that includes every tech entrepreneur, salon owner, and independent insurance representative from New York to Nairobi. Approximately 180 million of them are Christ followers. That's 180 million men and women who are creating and shaping culture; 180 million men and women who already know that their work is an opportunity to transform and innovate, to help and serve, to launch and learn; 180 million men and women who are just like you—who are building businesses on behalf of the God who made them.

Our vision is that in ten years, every Christ-following entrepreneur will know the majesty of the gospel first, and with that gift fully received, will be inspired to bring their gifting, experience, talent, and work to the altar as their meaningful form of spiritual worship, thereby transforming the workplaces, families, and communities in which they operate.

We want to see that happen in the lives of entrepreneurs all around the world. This is the mission that gets me out of bed every morning and that has motivated the writing of this book.

So, a number of us set out to determine the defining characteristics of a Faith Driven Entrepreneur—the values, habits, and traits that allow men and women to successfully build a business and faithfully pursue a loving relationship with their God. And that's what this book is. It's an outline of those characteristics, stories that display what they look like, and encouragement for how you can see them in your own life.

Along with this book, we've partnered with RightNow Media to produce videos that reinforce the principles described here. At the end of each chapter, we've included a suggested video that tells the story of a Faith Driven Entrepreneur that will help you further explore what that characteristic looks like as it's lived out. And at the end of the book, we've included a discussion guide that will help you dive deeper into these ideas with others. Because despite what you may have felt in the past, you don't have to go it alone.

This book is the starting line. It's not meant to be comprehensive or the final word on the subject. It's just the start—for me, for you, and for the entire Faith Driven Entrepreneur movement. So start reading. And more important, start realizing that God has a plan for every entrepreneur, and he's inviting you into it. Will you join?

CHAPTER 1

OUR CALL TO CREATE

Henry Kaestner

The word *calling* has dominated Christian circles in recent years, and it has taken on a mysterious power that no one seems to have nailed down. Does God call people into certain jobs and professions? Is calling a special spiritual experience? Are some people called and other people not? Questions abound, and we can debate all we want about what calling means and how we can discern our own, but the real harm in our conversations around calling is found in the spiritual caste system it has created between secular and sacred callings.

If you grew up in a Christian home in the last thirty to

forty years, maybe you've noticed that being "called" into ministry seems like a special, more elite, and more personal path than having a career in other professions. Christians often consider those called to vocational ministry a Special Ops group that only certain people are qualified for. We often believe that there are regular believers on one side and preachers, teachers, and missionaries on the other. And while we can't *all* be missionaries and preachers, it's easy to feel like those people have received something special from God that we haven't.

Or, if you're new to faith, you may be wondering if what you do in your professional life is illegitimate or a waste of time. If God has put us on this earth to love him and love others, and if our daily work isn't evangelistic in nature, do we need a new model? Reading about a lemonade-stand kid turned tech giant doesn't exactly scream "holy calling" to us.

But why not? Why can't an entrepreneurial venture, lived and pursued faithfully, be God's desire for your life?

I think it can be.

Entrepreneurs have a unique opportunity to step into a purpose that is aligned with who God is and how God has made them. Just as pastors are taking the gifts God has given them and giving those gifts back to others, entrepreneurs can take the creative problem-solving energy within them and pour that back out into society in a way that is beneficial to those who receive it and glorifying to the God who instilled it in them in the first place.

As an entrepreneur, you've felt the life-giving energy that comes through serving your customers, vendors, and investors. You get fired up when you find solutions to problems. You can't

> **Entrepreneurs have a unique opportunity to step into a purpose that is aligned with who God is and how God has made them.**

wait to see the fruit of the work of your hands. Why? Because you're created in the image of a creative, entrepreneurial God.

If you've ever felt less-than in the church because of your business, or if you've ever wondered whether your life is truly leaning into the purpose God has for you, look back at the Garden of Eden. God created humans in his image. And in his image, we can see a God who worked six days and created something out of nothing. That's who we are. That's what an entrepreneur does!

This is how it works. When you solve problems from scratch, that's an opportunity to commune with the living God who has helped people solve problems from the beginning of time.

When you provide a new idea, a new resource, or a new product, that's a chance to bear witness to a God who is the ultimate provider.

When you pray, "Thy kingdom come, thy will be done on earth as it is in heaven," God is answering that prayer with a resounding *yes*, and he's running toward you, eagerly inviting you to come under his power and his protection to join him in doing the work to make that happen.

Leave your feelings of inadequacy at the door. You were made for this. God has something incredible in store for the Faith Driven Entrepreneur.

>

A lot of images come to mind with the word *entrepreneur*. There's a Silicon Valley stereotype that includes a button-down shirt with a Patagonia vest. A lot of people will think of someone young, someone working in technology. Few people would think of a gardener.

But think about it. A gardener is nothing if not an entrepreneur. A gardener has the raw materials of soil and seeds and water, which they combine and tend in an effort to create something where, only days and weeks before, nothing existed. Beauty replaces nothingness; lush plants replace dry ground. What was once just a plot of land, a gardener turns around through the work of their hands and makes something useful—either for its aesthetic or for its function, and sometimes both.

And if we want to learn what it means to be a Faith Driven Entrepreneur, the first place we can look to is a garden. Because you, entrepreneur—whether you're calling yourself that yet or not—are a gardener. But you're not the first.

God is the original entrepreneur. If anyone knows what it's like to create and build something completely new, it's him. And we can see that from the very beginning he has created us to share in his entrepreneurial process: "The LORD God took the man and put him in the Garden of Eden to work it and take care of it" (Genesis 2:15).

God invited Adam into the work of caring for and cultivating the Garden right away. He didn't just set Adam down in Eden and tell him to enjoy himself. Adam had roles and responsibilities. You think your day is busy today? Imagine having to name every single animal in existence!

So often, we think of work as a curse—as something God made us do after we got kicked out of the Garden. But what if work is actually a part of bearing his image? What if work is an invitation to create and build alongside the ultimate entrepreneur? What if work is something God gave us as a vehicle through which we can enjoy his presence?

> **What made the Garden of Eden so special wasn't the absence of work. It was the presence of the perfect coworker.**

What made the Garden of Eden so special wasn't the absence of work. It was the presence of the perfect coworker. God and Adam worked together. The Garden of Eden and all the plants and animals in it were shared between God and man. That's the perfect vision of entrepreneurship—that we can be united in purpose, passion, and pursuit with God.

9

God wants to work with us. He wants to create with us. He wants to start, share, and complete new projects and ideas with us. He didn't leave Adam alone to tend to the Garden of Eden, and he doesn't ask us to work in isolation.

God uses us to bring about his Kingdom on earth as it is in heaven. Our creations can bring order out of chaos, solve problems, rally against injustice, and create dignity and opportunity for those who interact with our creations.

This truth should empower us. It should give us the ability to move forward confidently as we create and lead our businesses, as we propose solutions to societal problems, and as we step out in faith into the entrepreneurial venture God has drawn us to.

>

I discovered my first love when I went to college, and it was that I could buy a T-shirt for five dollars and sell it for ten dollars. As I did that, as I took risks and interacted with customers and thought about the next deal and saw the fruits of my labor as I hired other college students, I felt fully alive.

The creative process pumped blood into my veins. I came up with designs, made sales, and received affirmation from vendors and customers that I was doing a good thing. The feeling of validation that comes after creating something the market wants—even when that something was just a

T-shirt—was unbeatable. I was hooked. From my campus at the University of Delaware, we ended up selling on forty-nine other campuses up and down the East Coast.

Still, I put that aside as a collegiate venture. When I graduated, I thought I needed to get a real job. I moved to New York City and worked on Wall Street for six years. Now, you'd think that making a lot of money and living in New York City would be the dream. You'd think that would be better than selling T-shirts. But it wasn't. During that time, I longed for the entrepreneurial venture. I missed it. I wanted to feel fully alive again.

So I packed up and moved to North Carolina to start my own company. At the time, I had no perception of calling; I had no concept of what God wanted me to do with my life. I didn't think about things in a framework of faith at all. I was just chasing a bug to create and innovate.

And my bet is that if you're reading this book, you have that bug too. You want to break out of whatever societal box makes you feel trapped, and you want to move and shake and do and work and make something. That's the entrepreneurial dream. And since you're reading a book about being a *Faith Driven* Entrepreneur, my guess is you're serious about your Christian faith as well.

For far too long, Christian culture has ignored and dismissed this type of desire. I've met too many faithful people who ask me hesitantly, "Is it okay if I say no to working for

> **Entrepreneurship provides a place where you get to commune with God through the creative process.**

a church or missions agency and start a business instead?" They're cautious, uncertain, scared, and wondering if the entrepreneurial journey aligns with God's call for believers.

I'm here to tell you, yes. It absolutely does. Entrepreneurship provides a place where you get to commune with God through the creative process. It provides a way through which you can love God and love others. And so my hope is that as you read through the rest of these chapters—these marks of a Faith Driven Entrepreneur—you will feel empowered to do what you're doing and to do it well.

Entrepreneurship is a legitimate pursuit that, when done well, brings honor and glory to our entrepreneurial God. You can speak confidently about what you do, because God is in you and with you.

WANT TO SEE THIS LIVED OUT?

Visit the Faith Driven Entrepreneur website at www.faithdrivenentrepreneur.org/book-stories to watch "Not Dead Yet," the story of Saddleback Leather Company. While serving as a missionary and English instructor in Mexico, Dave Munson started a side business out of the back of his truck. Today, he and his wife, Suzette, own and operate a high-end leather goods business that has attracted a dedicated following for the beauty and quality of its products. Visit the URL to watch the full video and find thousands of other like-minded entrepreneurs going through the video study together.

CHAPTER 2

IDENTITY IN CHRIST

Henry Kaestner

When I moved to North Carolina to start a business, Tom, my best friend from college, encouraged me to check out a church. At the time, my wife, Kimberley, and I had wanted to explore the Christian faith, but we hadn't yet taken that step. But Tom had been faithfully witnessing to me for ten years—that's a long time.

I'll never forget what he told me. He said, "You have to decide. Jesus is either a liar, a lunatic, or Lord." I'll never forget that framework, made famous by C. S. Lewis. It made sense to me: a multiple-choice question with a limited number of conclusions. But even as he shared that with me, I shrugged it off.

We still ended up attending Church of the Good Shepherd, and that's where I heard pastor David Bowen talk about why he believed the Bible is true—why he believed that what it said about Jesus Christ was factually accurate. At the time, even though I was searching, I had no place for that idea in my mind. It just didn't make sense. But it got my wheels spinning. Had I given the question of who Jesus is as much preparation and research as I did a big investor meeting? If it's a question with longer-lasting impact, should I not give it *more* thought? When I get to the end of my life, what will God ask of me? How can I be prepared to answer? What if he asks me if I've read the Bible? And the scariest, what if he asks me if I know what it means? As I thought about it, I realized that if the Bible was what was going to keep me out of heaven, I had to give the book a shot.

So I tried it. And to tell you the truth, I didn't get very far. But I knew a thing or two about CliffsNotes from my time in school, and I looked at the back and thought that the New Testament seemed like a pretty good summary of what I wanted to know.

I read it, and I didn't buy it. My first time reading through the New Testament actually pushed me further away from faith. I just didn't see what was really going on.

But I decided to read it again, and my second time through, the Holy Spirit opened my heart and mind to receive the truth about God and Jesus and the relationship he desired to have with me. This changed everything.

>

Since that day, I've come to understand that Faith Driven Entrepreneurs live lives that have been transformed by the gospel of Christ. They have accepted the free gift of salvation and now view bringing God glory as their greatest and highest purpose.

You might read that and think that's obvious. Or maybe you think that's a little extreme. Maybe you can tolerate the idea of God, but making his glory the core of your life's purpose and identity? *That* sounds crazy.

I actually think that's the only way to live.

We've all lived and acted like this wasn't true, right? We've lived where our identity was in who we are, what we've done, how much we've accomplished. At least, I certainly did! And let me tell you, it just doesn't work.

> **Faith Driven Entrepreneurs have been transformed by the gospel of Christ. They view bringing God glory as their greatest and highest purpose.**

The ultimate satisfaction you're looking for in your business, your creation, your ideas, your profits—your whatever—is simply not there. When we place our identity in these things, we're pulling on the firmest Jenga blocks, begging for our lives to come crumbling down.

And if you're honest, you've probably already experienced this in some way or another.

There was a time when David Morken and I were seeking investors for our new company, Bandwidth, and we went 0 for 40 on pitches around Silicon Valley and elsewhere. No one wanted anything to do with what we had created. And as I look back on that time, I think, *If my identity was in myself, if I was the only one I depended on, I would've been crushed.* But my identity wasn't in my ability to attract investors. It wasn't in my ability to create a great business. I wanted those things—of course!—but they weren't at the core of who I was as a person.

Why? Because I knew who I was in God's eyes. I knew that when God looked at me, he saw his Son. I knew that my brokenness was made whole in Christ's perfection.

In addition to going 0 for 40 when we were first looking for investors for Bandwidth, I should also share that we sold our first company for $10 million. I say that not to congratulate myself, but to say that I've seen both the valleys and the mountaintops. And both are empty when you try to leave God out of the picture.

It's easy to be a hotshot or to have a god complex as an entrepreneur. When things are going great, we feel untouchable. But at the same time, it's easy to be terrified. If things aren't going well, we feel the crushing weight of responsibility. We get to experience both success and failure in their fullest forms—the highest of highs and the lowest of lows. But we don't have to experience them alone. And we don't have to depend on our circumstances to define our personhood.

When we understand that our deepest identity is as God's beloved children, we get to accept the gift of life given to us by Jesus Christ. Life then becomes more about being and less about doing—more about who we are in relationship to God and less about what we think we can do on our own. And when this reality sinks in, our gratitude for this amazing blessing fuels us to bring all that we are and all that we have to the altar of God as our meaningful act of worship. Paul says it best:

> Therefore, I urge you, brothers and sisters, in view of God's mercy, to offer your bodies as a living sacrifice, holy and pleasing to God—this is your true and proper worship. Do not conform to the pattern of this world, but be transformed by the renewing of your mind. Then you will be able to test and approve what God's will is—his good, pleasing and perfect will.
>
> ROMANS 12:1-2

There's clearly a pattern to this world. Maybe you've observed it, or you're stuck in it, or both. But a relationship with God offers you a way to break out of the vicious, self-serving cycle of independence and isolation that threatens to capture so many entrepreneurs today. Instead, he offers you a chance to put your identity in something outside of yourself and to live for another's glory.

>

If you want to live the life of a Faith Driven Entrepreneur, you can start by asking yourself a simple question: What is most important? This question, in fact, comes from the mouth of someone else—someone who had a chance to ask Jesus this very thing:

> One of the teachers of the law came and heard them debating. Noticing that Jesus had given them a good answer, he asked him, "Of all the commandments, which is the most important?"
>
> "The most important one," answered Jesus, "is this: 'Hear, O Israel: The Lord our God, the Lord is one. Love the Lord your God with all your heart and with all your soul and with all your mind and with all your strength.' The second is this: 'Love your neighbor as yourself.' There is no commandment greater than these."
>
> MARK 12:28-31

"Which is the most important?"

It's such a great question. And it's something we all want to know, right? What's the most important thing? When it comes to our work and our life, Jesus makes it simple: love God and love others.

What's the most important thing? When it comes to our work and our life, Jesus makes it simple: love God and love others.

As Faith Driven Entrepreneurs, we build our businesses, our lives, and our identities with these two commandments as our foundation. That being said, this doesn't mean that we have to pass out tracts in the office or engrave Bible verses or ichthus fish symbols on all our products. But it does mean that our heart posture is aligned with who God says we are and what he wants from us and for us, and our daily decisions flow from that reality.

It also means that it should be impossible for someone to spend any meaningful time with us and not know that our Christian faith is what guides and drives us. It's our faith that demands we do everything we do—heart, soul, mind, and strength—with love for God and love for others at the forefront.

One of our early investments at Sovereign's Capital was in a founder who had started a great young company, but after some shifts in the market, he found himself in a position where he had to lay off a lot of employees. There are lots of ways to fire people—books have been written on the subject. In fact, this entrepreneur started there, and the advice he found was to make the firing quick and clean. Just get it over with.

He walked into work the next day prepared to do just that, but as he prayed during his commute, God gave him a different idea. Instead of getting the layoff over as quickly as possible, he stood up in front of the entire company and admitted all of the mistakes he'd made that had led them to this position. He pointed out each of the errors, refusing to cast blame on those who didn't deserve it. And he explained how a layoff, as painful as it would be, was the only thing that would ensure the future of the organization.

That day the entire company set aside time to help those who were laid off move out of their offices, find leads for new jobs, and pray with them before they left. The company's leadership helped them update and share their résumés as well as wrote reviews for each employee on LinkedIn. It was difficult and messy, but it was how this entrepreneur's faith showed up that day.

This is what it looks like when your identity is in Christ: it means that every product, every aspect of the job, every relationship with partners, employees, suppliers, and customers works toward bringing about God's redemptive story.

You can choose that path.

Because the truth is that Jesus has already died for your sins. He has already defeated death and given you a chance to live eternally with him. The work is done.

Yet we're still here. So, we have to ask ourselves, How am I going to live in the extra time that God has given me?

Am I going to build up stores for myself while also trying to build myself up? Or am I going to realize that it's not about me at all?

We can strive and clench and grab and gain and control all day long. But there's no freedom in that form of ownership. The only way to experience life as an entrepreneur in the way God designed it is to place our entire identity in him and to view ourselves as stewards of whatever he has put in our hands.

WANT TO SEE THIS LIVED OUT?

Visit the Faith Driven Entrepreneur website at www.faithdrivenentrepreneur.org/book-stories to watch Phil Vischer, creator of *VeggieTales*, share the importance of keeping your business from becoming your identity. Visit the URL to watch the full video and find thousands of other like-minded entrepreneurs going through the video study together.

CHAPTER 3

STEWARDSHIP VS. OWNERSHIP

Chip Ingram

Early in my life as a Christian, I was a teacher making about $1,000 a month and had very few expenses. I had been discipled by some people who did a good job of teaching me how to have a quiet time, memorize verses, share my faith, and give the first portion of my income to God. Though I didn't necessarily have the right perspective on money, I was taught that tithing 10 percent, give or take a percentage point, was a good place to start.

I paid about $120 in rent (yeah, this was a long time ago!), so I had quite a bit of my monthly income left over. I decided I would increase my giving to 20 percent, then

30 percent. And I have to confess, I was a little pharisaical about it. Somehow I got the idea that the more I gave, the more spiritual I would be and the more God would love me. And I was pretty proud of my percentage.

Granted, 30 percent of a thousand dollars isn't very much, but I was impressed with my generosity. I even let it slip in conversation every once in a while so other people would be impressed too. I still didn't understand that it was all God's. I thought I was doing God a pretty big favor.

During this time, I owned a little green Volkswagen Beetle. It was my first car, and it was pretty cool. I liked it a lot.

After I married Theresa and we decided to move to Dallas for me to attend seminary, we had to figure out what to do with our cars. We could only take one, and she had recently bought a nice Chevy Nova. It made sense to take hers with us and to sell my Volkswagen. So I started thinking about how much I'd be able to get for my car.

A Volkswagen of that model, year, and condition was going for about $600. But I kept thinking I could get more for it. Maybe $800. Perhaps even $1,000, as a gas shortage at the time was making cars like mine more valuable every day. The dollar signs kept increasing in my own mind—until I was driving to work one morning.

I heard a still, small voice. *Chip, whose car is this?*

Surely that couldn't be God. I shifted my thoughts to the basketball practice I'd be leading later that day.

That voice came back the next day, and again the next. *Chip, whose car is this?*

I've realized over the years that when you get a strong impression over and over again, and it lines up with Scripture and has something to do with serving and loving other people, it's probably the Holy Spirit. But it took me a while to figure that out back then.

After about four days of denial, I answered, *This is your car, Lord.*

That's right, Chip. I have a plan for this car. I would realize later that he really had a plan for my heart.

So what's your plan for this car? I asked.

You know Nancy—your friend who's planning to be a Wycliffe missionary? You have two cars, right?

Yes.

She has no car, right?

I didn't like where this was going.

The voice continued, *She's moving to Southeast Asia to translate the Bible for a remote people who don't know me. She'll need to travel all over the United States to raise support, and she'll need to drive something that doesn't use a lot of gas. I want you to take that car of mine—the one I've let you use for six years—and give it to her.*

"You're kidding," I said out loud.

He wasn't kidding, of course.

I did what he said. Well, eventually. First I decided to

take my prized stereo out of the car before I gave it to Nancy. Theresa came out to the garage while I was pulling it out.

"What are you doing?" she asked.

"Well, you know, honey . . . God said the car, but I mean . . . my stereo, too?"

She put her hands on her hips and gave me a look.

"Okay," I mumbled and put the stereo back in.

I learned a lot from this incident. Please understand: I didn't obey God because I was naturally generous, noble, or godly. I did it simply because God said to. It was an obedience issue.

I also learned an invaluable lesson: I hadn't believed that everything I had really belonged to God. Even though I had been giving between 20 and 30 percent of my income, I had been doing it to impress myself, others, and God. I still hadn't made it to the first base in my understanding of stewardship, let alone the genius of generosity.

>

Generosity is a beautiful word, isn't it? It rolls off the tongue and conjures up images of joyful, extravagant giving and receiving.

Stewardship, on the other hand, sounds heavier and more serious to many people—like obligation and strict limits on spending.

Why? Because Christians and many other groups have

historically described stewardship in those narrow terms. But biblical stewardship is a beautiful thing because it's an amazing privilege that God has given to us.

Once a man named John Saville gave me a similar privilege. I met John in the first church I pastored in rural Texas. I was a young, inexperienced pastor with a lot of zeal and not much wisdom. John, by contrast, was an elderly man who had come to Christ late in life and had suffered some pretty hard knocks along the way. We had absolutely nothing in common except that he was the chairman of the elders and I was the new pastor of this not-so-thriving church of 35 people in a town of 3,500.

To be candid, I thought John was a little kooky at first. He had simple answers for my "complex" questions. He quoted Galatians 2:20 or Oswald Chambers as the answer to almost everything. On top of that, he said "praise the Lord" a lot, which was very uncool in my mind.

There was absolutely no reason for John and me to see each other except for a once-a-month elders' meeting, let alone to become best friends, as we later did—apart from the genius of generosity.

One day John asked me to drive into Dallas to have lunch with him at the downtown accounting firm he owned. He told me to wear a tie because the restaurant required it.

I'll never forget how intimidated I was as I traveled up the glass building's elevator to his wood-paneled reception area.

My middle-class roots were deeply challenged as we dined on the top floor overlooking all of Dallas. It was a world I had never experienced, and John seemed particularly thrilled to treat me to the best he could offer. He insisted that I get the filet—"Best steak around," he assured me.

Toward the end of lunch, this grand old man pulled a small white box from his coat pocket and told me he had a proposition that he wanted me to consider. He called it a business deal of sorts. Not a business deal to make money, but a business deal to give it away. John gave me a three-point outline as he laid out what he called our "Secret Pact":

1. I have a desire to help poor and hurting people.
2. You are in contact with poor and hurting people daily.
3. I want you to be my eyes and ears and help them as God leads you.

With that, John reached into the box, pulled out a brown checkbook, and handed it to me. As I opened it, I saw the words "pastor's discretionary fund" neatly printed on the front. The deposit ledger in the back had a five and three zeros neatly printed in the far right column.

I looked up at this loving, kooky man and said, "Do you mean you want me to figure out who to help and then help them the way you would if you saw the situation, Mr. Saville?"

John smiled and said, "That's exactly what I want you to do, Chip!"

Five thousand dollars, five thousand dollars . . . My head was swimming as I repeated that number over and over, riding down the elevator to get in my old unair-conditioned car in the ninety-eight-degree Dallas summer heat. John had sworn me to secrecy, and thus began a series of divine lessons that only later would I recognize as the genius of generosity.

What was I to John? His steward, of course. And it was wonderful to play that role! It was an exciting adventure to give away the $5,000 to those in need around me. Instead of it feeling like a chore or a boring obligation, it was a thrilling honor. Though it was challenging at times to make wise decisions that would faithfully represent John's wishes, writing those checks was one of the most joyful experiences I'd had in my entire life.

But here's the thing: everyone has the same opportunity! We are all God's stewards. And stewardship is a key part of why generosity is so genius.

True generosity flows out of an understanding that God owns everything—and I mean *everything*. We're working with God's goods. We're the cooks in his kitchen. That's the honest, humbling truth. Even, and perhaps especially, if you started your own business, you're creating out of the ingredients God created first.

In God's economy, good stewardship is by nature generous

> **If we want to understand generosity biblically, we need to see stewardship through new lenses— less as a reluctant obligation and more as an exciting opportunity.**

and joyful. It directs his resources extravagantly toward his purposes and for his people to deeply enjoy. If we want to understand generosity biblically, we need to see stewardship through new lenses—less as a reluctant obligation and more as an exciting opportunity.

I know this may be old news for you. The Bible makes it clear that God owns everything (see Psalm 50:12)— that however much we give back to him financially, the rest belongs to him too. But even though we have been taught that truth and intellectually accept it, most of us do not live as though we believe it's true.

Instead, we act as owners, like things belong to us. This is a tempting way to live because it puts control and power in our hands. But that's just our pride talking. Stewards understand that anything in their hands has been put there by God and is to be used for his glory. Stewardship isn't just a spiritual exercise or a test of obedience. There's a bigger purpose behind it.

It's one thing to believe everything we have and everything we are belongs to God. It's another for that truth to sink down into our hearts where we feel it and grasp it. And when it really sinks down, all the way into our gut where it shapes everything we think and feel and do, our lives are transformed.

We shift from simply having theoretical knowledge to experiencing the genius of generosity. We move from duty to delight; from rules we keep to an adventure we share. We wake up in the morning wondering what we are going to do with God's time or how we are going to spend his money. We think about how we are going to relate to the spouse and kids he has entrusted to us or the friends he has placed in our lives.

When we turn ownership over to God, we are freed from the pressures of performance and we experience joy from working alongside God. What could be better than that?

The point I want to emphasize with this principle is not that God owns everything and we're his stewards. The deeper issue is trust—a relational issue. A steward must be found trustworthy. God has entrusted to us everything we have for a reason—so we can partner with him to accomplish his purposes and so we can demonstrate where our true priorities lie.

Jesus tells us in Luke 16 that if we're faithful in small things—handling money, for example—we will be entrusted with greater things. But if we're not trustworthy in small things, then we won't be trustworthy with greater things. How we handle our money, our talents, our businesses, and so on determines, to a large degree, what God blesses us with spiritually and eternally. In other words, learning to give wisely and to steward our worldly wealth is foundational. It's like the ABCs of faithfulness, a first step. If we don't get that down, we don't move on very far.

But if we do, we step into whole new areas of blessing and opportunity. We get true riches, the kind that allow us to play a role in transforming other lives and impacting souls. We receive eternal treasures.

>

As a pastor for over thirty years, I've had scores of conversations with sincere Christians who can't understand why they're experiencing so little of God's power and seeing so little happen in their lives. When I ask a few questions, I usually discover they have never connected the dots between their use of money and God's activity and blessing in their lives and significant relationships.

So I tell them that there's a better, smarter way to live . . . an idea so simple, it's genius. It's a generous life of stewardship.

Faithful stewards are mindful of the one they represent. Not only are they good managers of their master's money and resources, they know who their master is. Good stewards learn how to direct their master's resources entrusted to them. Like me, learning what made John's spirits soar, we can learn what brings exceeding joy to Christ.

To be that kind of steward—insightful managers growing in an understanding of God's generosity and learning to be generous like him—we need to ask three questions regularly:

1. Am I using everything entrusted to me in accordance with the owner's wishes?

When you look at your checking account, your bank statements, your investments, and everything else in your financial profile, do you see a clear direction toward fulfilling God's purposes and his agenda? Or do you see them focused on fulfilling your own agenda?

When you look at how you approach your customers, your employees, and your vendors, are you treating them as objects under your control or as people under God's umbrella of grace and love?

God has a plan and purpose for every man, woman, and child. We can see some clear themes in Scripture.

One is the great commission. God is concerned about every lost person on this planet. He wants them to hear the gospel and to come to know Jesus personally. If your energy is going toward reaching lost people, it's going toward his purposes.

A second key purpose is building up the body of Christ, the church. God wants every believer to grow to spiritual maturity and to fulfill their purpose in him. When we work toward that end, we are using his resources for his purposes.

Third, God is passionate about hurting, desperate people. He is compassionate toward those in need. If we put our resources into acts of compassion and justice for those who have deep physical, emotional, and spiritual needs, our giving is aligned with his purposes.

We can know we are being trustworthy in fulfilling God's wishes when we are putting his resources toward these things.

2. Am I carefully keeping an account of where the owner's goods are going?

Whether we're giving God 10 percent or 50 percent, whatever's left after our offering is still his. We're just as accountable for how we spend the remaining 90 percent or the remaining 50 percent as we are for giving him the first and best to start with. This applies not only to money but to our time and talent as well.

To do that, we have to keep track of where everything is being spent. Think of it like a budget. One of the clearest pieces of evidence that we are serious about being good money managers is that we live on at least some semblance of a budget. It's impossible to be a good steward of someone else's money if we haven't determined where it will go and tracked it along the way.

The majority of people don't live on a budget. We pay the bills and then spend the rest somewhat randomly or without clear intentions.

When we view ourselves as owners, it's easy to be careless—or worse, selfish—with what God has entrusted to us. Instead, we need to understand the business God has given us, the people God has put under us, and the customers he has brought to us to serve and view all of those things as "budget items" for which we are accountable.

Where are you spending most of your time and energy? Where are you spending most of your money? Who do these efforts and expenditures benefit?

These are hard questions to ask, but they'll at least get you started down a path of understanding whether you truly view yourself as an owner or a steward, and they'll guide you closer to becoming the latter.

3. Am I becoming best friends with the owner while managing his resources?

Though a lot of faithful stewardship involves sacrifice, don't let that overshadow the joy of fulfilling your Father's wishes and celebrating your fruitfulness with him. There's nothing legalistic in the kind of stewardship we're talking about. We're becoming faithful stewards because we want to, not simply because we have a duty or we want God to love us more. He'll never love us more than he loves us right now.

My relationship with John only deepened over the time we spent working together. We went from acquaintances who saw each other once a month to coworkers and friends who were challenging each other to see how God could move in and through us. Meeting together to talk through how I was stewarding his money was never a task to accomplish. It was a joy. It was exhilarating.

Generous giving and faithful stewardship create an opportunity for us to enjoy God's blessing and delight. That's part of the genius of generosity: it deepens our relationship with him. Have a few extravagant lunches with him to celebrate what you and he have done together with his resources.

> **Stewardship is not about depriving yourself. It's enjoying God's generosity for yourself and then sharing it with others.**

"The earth is the LORD's, and everything in it," says God's Word (Psalm 24:1), and he loves it when we celebrate with him—guilt-free. Stewardship is not about depriving yourself. It's enjoying God's generosity for yourself and then sharing it with others. It's living under the gaze of an infinite being who loves you and says, "First and foremost, give it and spend it in a way that's pleasing to me and that acknowledges I own it all. Manage it well. Then, let's celebrate. Let's rejoice. I am your Father. I love you. Every good and perfect gift comes from my hand to bless and encourage you. Let me delight over you and your faithfulness."

That's what stewardship is about.

Your life will be drastically transformed when you realize,

deep down, that everything belongs to God, and he trusts you to use it well.

Wake up every day asking, *Lord, what do you want me to do with this time, talent, and treasure you've given me? What would make you happiest and give me the most bang for my buck spiritually? What can I do to become better friends with you through this process—to get to the place where we can have extravagant lunches and celebrate your goodness, and where I can feel your pleasure over me?*

Thinking like a faithful and generous steward will produce great joy and fruitfulness in your life. Enjoy God's generosity to you, then share it with others so you can all enjoy him together.

WANT TO SEE THIS LIVED OUT?

Visit the Faith Driven Entrepreneur website at www.faithdrivenentrepreneur.org/book-stories to watch Pete Ochs, CEO of Seat King, talk about how a new understanding of generosity and stewardship changed his business and his life. Visit the URL to watch the full video and find thousands of other like-minded entrepreneurs going through the video study together.

CHAPTER 4

IN PARTNERSHIP

Henry Kaestner

Frodo isn't the hero of The Lord of the Rings.

It's true. I know he carries the ring all the way to Mordor, bearing the burden that no other man, elf, or dwarf could endure. But he's not the hero.

We find out who the real hero is at the end of *The Fellowship of the Ring*. Frodo has carried the ring for the entire story so far, but he realizes that he doesn't want to take his friends into the danger and doom that await him. So he tries to take one of the boats and sneak away.

But Sam figures out what Frodo is going to do and catches him in the act of leaving. In desperation, Sam hurls himself at the boat to join Frodo, but he misses and, unable to swim, begins to sink.

Of course, Frodo saves Sam. The two get into the boat, and you can read the rest of the story for yourself. But it's this act of complete selflessness that defines the journey that Frodo and Sam embark on together. Frodo does everything possible to fulfill his duty, bearing as much responsibility as he can, but Sam never lets him do it alone. Sam never leaves his side. He never abandons his partner and friend.

That's what makes Samwise Gamgee the hero of the story. Sam, the loyal steward and best friend of Frodo, is the only reason the One Ring to rule them all makes it all the way to Mordor. Through every up and down, twist and turn, Sam is there to advance the mission and to keep the goal of safely returning home in sight.

The results and outcomes rest on the shoulders of the business leader. But doing it alone is a fool's game.

Frodo was brave, but he was nothing without Sam. He never would have made it alone.

This story, to me, encapsulates the importance of having a great business partner. The journey of an entrepreneur is a lonely one. The results and outcomes rest on the shoulders of the business leader. But doing it alone is a fool's game.

>

I have philosophical and practical reasons for believing in partnership. Philosophically, I believe God designed us to be in relationship with other people. Whether you look at Matthew 18:20, where Jesus says, "Where two or three gather in my name, there am I with them," or at the idea from Ecclesiastes 4:12 that "a cord of three strands is not quickly broken," there's no denying the power of community and the fact that God intended us to work together.

This is not to mention the fact that Jesus, the Son of God, surrounded himself with twelve disciples. He wasn't a lone missionary wandering from town to town. He was in a group, both helping and being helped, working with others toward the common goal of bringing the Good News to the world.

It's a powerful example to follow, and I look back on my own life and marvel at the impact my business partners have had on me.

In my experience with Chapel Hill Brokers and Tom Hahn, then with Bandwidth and David Morken, and today Sovereign's Capital with Luke Roush, there's no way I would have been able to accomplish any of the things we did had I tried to do them alone. It's a cliché that one plus one equals three, but it often does when it comes to partnering with great people.

And while partnership in general is powerful, the shared faith and shared mission that Faith Driven Entrepreneurs can have with their business partners brings out even more from this dynamic. A healthy partnership founded on shared faith and shared mission can be a model for the rest of the employees, partners, vendors, and customers of what it means to work together as a team. I've seen that. I've witnessed how people have valued my partnerships with others, and that has helped our company to land and keep and grow accounts. Others trust us because of the healthy partnership at the core of the business. I've seen it impact the way we inspire and encourage our employees.

This brings up the idea of a "united front," which is something that comes up in a lot of parenting books. The idea is that parents want their children to see them as a unit, as two people who are on the same page. In a way, the same principle applies to business partners.

While I'm not suggesting that you require everyone on your staff or senior management team to share your faith, having a business partner who is "equally yoked" (see 2 Corinthians 6:14) with you in terms of faith and mission is invaluable. When it's necessary to make tough decisions about staying on mission, even when such a decision may hurt the bottom line, you will be grateful to have a partner who shares your priorities and values. Not only that, but you'll be grateful to have someone there with you as you process decisions together.

This is how culture is formed. It's how your employees come to work with a sense of security, knowing that the leaders of the company are on the same page, working toward the same goals.

And lastly, while we're on the philosophical side of the idea of partnership, having a great business partner is a key part of being able to fully experience the joy of entrepreneurship. It's possible to have joy as a sole proprietor, but the value of shared experience cannot be overstated. There's infinitely more joy that can be had by going through the jungle, through the desert, through battle with somebody else by your side.

If you're married, you may already get to experience that with your spouse. When it comes to a business partner—someone you spend the majority of your day with—this same sense of camaraderie and companionship can be incredibly life-giving.

>

Now, in terms of the practical, a business partner is crucial to getting even the simplest things done.

In the early days when David and I were pitching investors on Bandwidth, we were able to tag team that effort. We would present at different business meetings, and while I was talking, he was reading the room. And when he started talking, I did the same. Then after the meeting, we would compare notes and have a better understanding of how it went and how we could improve. We were able to adjust and say, "You should do this next time" or "Maybe we should try something different here." It was a powerful and obvious way where having someone in that meeting with me, in those same trenches, made all the difference in the world.

It was such a powerful experience that now, as an investor, I look to invest in partners. A partnership isn't the only business model, by any means, but from my vantage point, it's preferred. It's impossible for me to imagine going through the highs and lows of starting a business alone. While I know that many sole proprietors have been doing this for decades, I also know that the ones living healthy lives have surrounded themselves with partners in the form of a faithful community.

> **Partnership demands ultimate transparency and vulnerability. Having a business partner builds these things into your daily work.**

Partnership demands ultimate transparency and vulnerability. Having a business partner builds these things into your daily work. When you're leading a business by yourself, you're constantly trying to present circumstances that best encourage your customers, your employees, your investors, and your spouse or other family members. And each of those is like a plate that's on fire that you have to keep spinning. It's exhausting.

Sharing that burden with someone is key. Having a partner you can turn to and just be honest with changes the way you approach business. When things are great, they share the joy of achievement. And when things are terrible, they're the one person that you don't have to convince that things aren't as bad as they look.

Your partner gets to know the inner workings of the business as well as you do. And when that type of professional transparency occurs, it can lead to a deeper personal vulnerability that is like a salve for your soul.

I mentioned my three business partners Tom, David, and Luke, and today those guys are my three best friends. We shared experiences that were so unique to our situations and circumstances that we forged bonds that will never be broken. I wanted to think of a story that encapsulates the importance of having a business partner, but truth be told, there isn't just one. Every experience we shared starting those businesses was great for just that reason—we *shared* it. The good, the bad, and the disagreements were things we took in stride together.

I look back on the early days, and they weren't all rainbows and sunshine. We had hard times, and there were moments when I strongly disagreed with my business partners. But for us, that was a part of the process. That was iron sharpening iron. Good arguments based on merit are the furnace that prepares the metal so you can shape it into whatever you want it to be.

We weren't beating each other down; we were pushing each other to be the best entrepreneurs, husbands, fathers, sons, friends, and men that we could be. That was our shared calling in Christ.

Secular entrepreneurs sometimes have irreconcilable differences, but that shouldn't happen to two business partners united in a faithful pursuit of Christ. Of course, that's not to say that all Christian partnerships will work perfectly. But when I look at my relationship with David, especially, I see two men who have different skill sets, different strengths, and different weaknesses. That worked to our advantage only because we were completely unified around our purpose in life and a sense of real truth.

What made us able to fulfill the shared mission we were working toward was a deeper understanding that a greater force was at work. We believed in bringing about God's Kingdom on earth as it is in heaven, and that brought us together better than anything else could have.

One of the most unifying experiences in life is to go through a battle with another human being. And business is a battle. It's hard work. It's challenging. Each day brings its own difficulties. But those trenches can create an unbreakable sense of unity that can be used to bring joy, purpose, and practical benefit to your life and your work.

>

We started this chapter talking about The Lord of the Rings, so it's only fitting to bring Tolkien back in here at the close. Many people have heard of the Inklings—the famous group of authors that included C. S. Lewis, J. R. R. Tolkien, Charles

Williams, and others. And perhaps the best known of those friendships is the one between Lewis and Tolkien, two names that are practically inseparable today.

But if you look back at these men's lives, to before Oxford and the Inklings, you'll find their first shared experience occurred in World War I. Both Lewis and Tolkien fought in the trenches of the Somme Valley in France, where they watched their friends die and experienced the brutal realities of war firsthand. And when you read their books, particularly The Lord of the Rings, you can see the effect this had on their lives and their writing.

The whole Lord of the Rings trilogy is centered around a group, a band of brothers, that was on the quest of all quests. There is the partnership of Sam and Frodo, of course, but you also get to follow the trio of Legolas, Gimli, and Aragorn and the pair of Merry and Pippin.

These relationships are so important in the books that you can envision Tolkien thinking about the friends with whom he went to war—the way those relationships, those partnerships were emblazoned on his very core. And while I don't mean to suggest that starting a business is the same as fighting in the trenches of World War I, the idea of a shared experience is there, and it's available for anyone willing to partner with someone else. Because business is its own battle. And the people you're fighting alongside will forever define your experience.

Today, the Faith Driven Entrepreneur ministry hosts

gatherings where entrepreneurs can come together and discuss life in the trenches. Hundreds of men and women—from Silicon Valley to South Africa, Atlanta to Jakarta, and everywhere in between—gather regularly to share in the highs and the lows of one another's work because we know what each of the others is going through. We share these experiences. Lewis and Tolkien had their original Inklings, where some of literature's greatest works were published through the prodding, probing, arguing, and encouragement of friends.

Faith Driven Entrepreneurs have that opportunity as well. We have the chance to link arms with someone who shares a relationship with Christ and who wants to see Christ's name glorified in all things. When that motivation lies behind two or more people leading a business, there's no limit to where the work can go.

That's the power of partnership. That's the power of working together with a shared faith toward a common goal.

WANT TO SEE THIS LIVED OUT?

Visit the Faith Driven Entrepreneur website at www.faithdrivenentrepreneur.org/book-stories to watch Henry Kaestner and David Morken, cofounders of Bandwidth, talk about how their partnership helped create a company culture they were proud of. Visit the URL to watch the full video and find thousands of other like-minded entrepreneurs going through the video study together.

CHAPTER 5

DON'T WORSHIP WORK

J. D. Greear

In middle school, Alex and Peter launched their first entrepreneurial enterprise, a little neighborhood project called "Dirt Cheap Lawn Care."

After their ninth grade summer, they were both over it, but for different reasons.

Alex saw his work as a necessary evil, little more than a means to score some cash to go to the arcade, see the occasional movie, and upgrade his wardrobe from his mom's unrelenting poor choices. Because work for Alex was merely a means to an end, he got little pleasure from it. He did the least he could to earn a buck. He cut corners. He was always pushing Peter to raise prices and offered little to no perks for loyal customers.

Peter, by contrast, loved the company. He felt more alive in it than he ever had. He loved the praise that came from his parents and satisfied customers, and he loved the status that came from being a high school student with a thriving business and plenty of cash. Peter buried himself in Dirt Cheap, because in *its* success he saw *his* success. The work was hard now, but he figured real, lasting happiness was just around the corner, the prize for an extra $1,000 in revenue. As he entered his sophomore year, however, he was dismayed that the girls at school seemed to care more about wavy hair and who scored the most points in the basketball game than about his thriving business. *Just a little bit more money, a little bit more success,* he thought, *and they'll see.*

Alex and Peter continued their business on into their thirties, and then it all fell apart. Alex simply hated being at work and couldn't believe he had stayed as long as he had. Peter could never round the corner into real happiness. Though he still loved the concept of running a business, he concluded that managing a lawn care business would not deliver the satisfaction and status he craved.

Alex and Peter represent the two key ways we can go wrong with our entrepreneurial work. Alex, you could say, was *idle.* Peter had made his work an *idol.*

My guess, based on the fact that you picked up this book, is that you identify more with Peter than with Alex. Many of us entered entrepreneurial work to find a sense of satisfaction, meaning, and significance. Eventually, though, we all realize we can't find those things there. Unfortunately, for many, by the time they realize it, the damage has been done. Consider these sobering statistics:

> **Many of us entered entrepreneurial work to find a sense of satisfaction, meaning, and significance. Eventually, though, we all realize we can't find those things there.**

- Entrepreneurs are two times more likely to suffer from depression.
- Entrepreneurs are three times more likely to battle some form of substance abuse.
- Entrepreneurs are two times more likely to have suicidal thoughts.
- Entrepreneurs are two times more likely to be hospitalized for psychiatric problems.[1]

There's a cost to placing all of our time, energy, and efforts exclusively in one place. Entrepreneurship, even when done in healthy partnership, is still an inherently lonely journey. After all, no matter how much people say they're "with you," no one else can take your risks, make your decisions, determine your values, or set your precedents. *You're* the one doing all that. That's a lot of weight on one set of shoulders.

I can't think of a more fitting book of the Bible to address this struggle than the book of Ecclesiastes. The majority of Ecclesiastes is written by Solomon, a man with incalculable wealth, world-renowned wisdom, unmatched power, and a list of accomplishments to put anyone to shame. And yet Solomon explained that *even with all that*, life often felt like *hevel*—a Hebrew word that literally means "vapor" or "smoke." His success felt like a cloud: from afar it might look solid, but when you pressed into it, you would discover it was vapor.

>

Solomon identifies four areas of life that disappoint us, not *in spite* of our successes but *because* of them. Entrepreneurs today need to keep a close eye on each of these four areas, lest our well-intended efforts become *hevel*, an impressive-looking cloud . . . full of nothing.

1. Pleasure ultimately disappoints.

Solomon writes, "Whatever my eyes desired I did not keep from them. I kept my heart from no pleasure" (Ecclesiastes 2:10, ESV). The man wasn't kidding, either. Everything in Solomon's house was made of gold. He feasted on the richest and most exotic foods from around the world. He took for himself a thousand wives and concubines to satisfy his every desire. (If that sounds like a bad idea to you—both practically and morally—I agree. But it shows just how far he was able to go to get *whatever* he wanted.) Solomon's kingdom, the nation of Israel, was at peace, larger and more powerful than it ever had been or ever would be.

But Solomon wasn't just a rich guy who happened to have a ton of money. He was also preternaturally talented. He was so well read that kings and queens from other nations marveled at his knowledge. He wrote *New York Times* bestselling books on every subject imaginable. He built the most impressive temple the world had ever seen. He even wrote songs that have endured for millennia.

Having done all this, what was Solomon's verdict? "Then I considered all that my hands had done and the toil I had expended in doing it, and behold, all was vanity and a striving after wind, and there was nothing to be gained under the sun" (Ecclesiastes 2:11, ESV).

In other words, "I tried to have it all. I succeeded. And it was completely, utterly empty."

Hevel. Vapor. Smoke.

2. Even the best business wisdom sometimes fails.

Here's Solomon again: "I saw that under the sun the race is not to the swift, nor the battle to the strong, nor bread to the wise, nor riches to the intelligent, nor favor to those with knowledge, but time and chance happen to them all" (Ecclesiastes 9:11, ESV).

Sometimes you do everything right and things just don't work out. You take a calculated risk, but the timing is off, so your venture falls flat. You reach out to everyone in your network to help a new business off the ground, but they're tied up with other projects and unable to help. An unforeseen event changes the market, and what once seemed like a sure thing suddenly becomes shaky.

Every entrepreneur knows that individual choices matter. This is why you read all the best books on leadership or creativity or marketing. You know that, by and large, wise business practices win out over foolish ones.

But that general principle isn't an ironclad law. Sometimes life just feels, well, *unlucky*. And when (not *if*, but *when*) that happens—when your wise business practices don't automatically lead to success—your whole life doesn't have to crumble. Instead, you can understand that God's wisdom and God's plan are better than anything we could come up with.

3. In the same way, worldly justice systems eventually fail us.

This one is even more troubling, because it's not just a matter of bad timing or bad luck. It's a matter of injustice. As Solomon notes, "There is something else meaningless that occurs on earth: the righteous who get what the wicked deserve, and the wicked who get what the righteous deserve. This too, I say, is meaningless" (Ecclesiastes 8:14).

We've all wrestled with this painful reality at some point. Sometimes on this earth good goes unrewarded and evil goes unpunished. Even worse, there are times when evil not only goes *unpunished* but seems to be *rewarded* as a path to success.

Should we hold people accountable for injustices in business? Absolutely. Insofar as it lies within our power, we should not only model integrity but also insist on integrity all around us. But we also have to acknowledge what Solomon knew: corruption often wins. And if our entire worth is built on our entrepreneurship, that reality threatens everything.

4. The fruit of our labor crumbles.

Solomon writes, "I hated all the things I had toiled for under the sun, because I must leave them to the one who comes after me. And who knows whether that person will be wise or foolish? Yet they will have control over all the fruit of my toil into which I have poured my effort and skill under the sun. This too is meaningless" (Ecclesiastes 2:18-19).

We've seen that happen through history with kingdoms, personal fortunes, sports teams, and business succession plans. It takes a lot of skill and wisdom to build something fruitful. It takes surprisingly little to undo it.

We may (and we should) think through succession plans.

We may (and we should) codify our values in our institutions so that they outlast us. We may (and we should) raise up leaders to carry on what we've built. But there are no guarantees. One day, like it or not, we will have to take our hands off our enterprises.

>

You may be a little uncomfortable with everything I've written so far. It's not that you disagree with Solomon's wisdom. But you've heard this kind of reasoning used to justify an amoral (or immoral) approach to life. After all, if nothing we do lasts, and if justice can fail us, then why care about doing the right thing? Why not just live it up and leave the mess for someone else to clean up?

Fortunately for us, Solomon doesn't go that route. Life may seem like *hevel*, but if we step back just a bit further, Solomon encourages us to see a bigger picture—one in which we *gladly* realize that entrepreneurship can't deliver satisfaction, meaning, or significance, because we already have those things in Christ.

Here are Solomon's four truths to help you avoid the dangers of entrepreneurial *hevel*.

1. Realize that you were created for God!

St. Augustine said it over 1,500 years ago: "Our hearts are restless until they find their rest in [God]." Satisfaction, meaning, and significance are not found in success. They are found only in our identity as God's children. When we root ourselves in that identity, the vicissitudes of life can only push us around so much. Success will still feel great; failure will still feel terrible. But with a firm anchor in Christ, success cannot intoxicate us, nor can failure devastate us.

The book of Ecclesiastes ends with Solomon realizing that the only thing left for us to do, in light of all that is meaningless, is to fear God and keep his commandments. Our relationship with God and our life that flows from it matter above everything else.

2. Arrange your life around the certainty of judgment.

Death and the judgment of God are two of the only absolute realities in your life. That judgment could come for you this afternoon; it could come in seventy years. But come it will.

We all want to ignore this reality, because let's face it: *it's not fun to meditate on death*. But uncomfortable realities don't simply disappear when we ignore them. In fact, they become even more dangerous.

There's a great (and startling) analogy for this that I've heard attributed to seventeenth-century French philosopher Blaise Pascal. He describes life as a giant party, full of happy people, loud music, and dancing, during which a monster unexpectedly bursts through the doors, grabs a random partygoer, mauls them in front of everyone, and drags their bloody corpse out of the room. Everyone watches in horror, and after it's over, they stare at one another in stunned silence for a few moments.

But then the band kicks back up and everyone returns to their frivolity, putting the horrendous display out of their minds. This horror is repeated every few moments until it becomes apparent that the monster is eventually coming for everyone in the room. Yet still the party goes on.

That monster, Pascal said, is our impending death.

This reality shouldn't terrify us. For believers, we know what lies on the other side of death. But it should sober us and moderate our expectations in life. We have only a short time on this earth. And only a fool would live as if he were going to live forever. So, as Solomon says, know how to count your days, and then make your days count.

3. Decide what God wants from you and pursue it.

And when I say "pursue it," I mean really go after it. Be willing to take a chance on it. Could you fail? Certainly. But God delights in those who risk greatly for him. That's as true in business as it is in missions.

Solomon writes, "Whoever watches the wind will not plant; whoever looks at the clouds will not reap" (Ecclesiastes

11:4). Here you have a farmer who never sows his seed because he is so scared the weather will not cooperate. *What if it doesn't rain? What if there is a sandstorm? An earthquake? A meteor shower?*

As we've seen throughout Ecclesiastes, Solomon acknowledges that we can't control things, and there is nothing in life that guarantees success—not great skill, careful planning, or even righteous living. You have to embrace that truth *and still work with wisdom and planning.* Solomon writes just a couple verses later, "Sow your seed in the morning, and at evening let your hands not be idle, for you do not know which will succeed, whether this or that" (Ecclesiastes 11:6). In other words, don't let the uncertainty of life and the possibility of failure paralyze you.

> **We can't control things, and there is nothing in life that guarantees success. We have to embrace that truth *and still work with wisdom and planning.***

In this life, nothing is guaranteed, even if you do it right. But risk is okay. Not all risk, mind you. Not foolish and reckless risk. But some risk is right and wise, even inevitable.

If we, as entrepreneurs, want an ironclad divine promise of success, we're just not guaranteed that in life. But that's not supposed to discourage us from taking wise, well-calculated risks.

4. Seek happiness in the present, not the future.

Solomon explains that we have a real temptation to always try to find happiness "out there." But happiness is not around the next corner. It's a gift from God for the present. You should look for it now, not later. If you're not happy, Solomon says it's not primarily a problem with your circumstances but with your relationship with God. "Now all has been heard; here is the conclusion of the matter: Fear God and keep his commandments, for this is the duty of all mankind" (Ecclesiastes 12:13). That's it. After everything that Solomon talked about, his conclusion is that we are to look to God, to fear him and obey him in the time we have.

Pascal, in his *Pensées*, said that the tragedy of many successful people is they never actually learn to enjoy life, because they are always living to enjoy it later. He writes,

> We never keep to the present. . . . We are so unwise
> that we wander about in times that do not belong
> to us, and do not think of the only one that does; so
> vain that we dream of times that are not and blindly
> flee the only one that is. . . . Let each of us examine
> his thoughts; he will find them wholly concerned
> with the past or the future. We almost never think of
> the present, and if we do think of it, it is only to see
> what light it throws on our plans for the future. The

present is never our end. The past and the present are our means, the future alone our end. *Thus we never actually live, but hope to live, and since we are always planning how to be happy, it is inevitable that we should never be so.*[2]

For the believer, that need not be true. God has good things in store for his children—not only in the future, but today.

>

A few years ago, the opportunity came up for me to be the president of the Southern Baptist Convention. I was legitimately excited about it. Now, I'd like to say that all my excitement was about how great of an opportunity this was to leverage a role for the advancement of the gospel. A lot of it was. But I was also excited by the newness of it. Here was a new challenge and a new platform, both of which whispered to my heart, *Perhaps* this *is the opportunity that will make you happy.*

During this time, my wife, Veronica, told me something incredibly helpful regarding fame. She said, "Fame is making yourself accessible to a bunch of people you don't know about at the expense of those you do." I realized she was right. My quality of life is better when I am available to people close to me, and newer and bigger exploits can sometimes take me away from them. That's not to say God doesn't call me to

> **The greatest gain God can give you is not more stuff or a new challenge or a bigger platform. The greatest gain he can give you is the ability to enjoy what you have.**

that sometimes (in the end, I took the role), just that I shouldn't be deceived about where happiness comes from.

Even in earthly terms, happiness, Solomon says, comes from the quality of relationships in the present, not the quantity of exploits in the future.

I point this out because I fear that many entrepreneurs will look around at their lives many years later and realize they gave away their greatest moments to get to some elusive future that didn't deliver what it offered. The apostle Paul says, "Godliness with contentment is great gain" (1 Timothy 6:6). The greatest gain God can give you is not more stuff or a new challenge or a bigger platform. The greatest gain he can give you is the ability to enjoy what you have.

Centuries after King Solomon, another powerful man rose to power. By the time he was in his twenties, he had conquered an empire astronomically larger than Solomon's—around two million square miles, nearly twice the size of modern India. He established cities that would last until the present day. Despite being a military man all his life, he never lost a battle. We know him today as Alexander the Great.

Alexander might have conquered more of the world than anyone else. But still he was unsatisfied, wishing for "another world to conquer." He worshiped his empire, and it made him miserable.

Don't be like Alexander. Submit your entrepreneurship to God and be excellent at it, *but don't turn it into a god.* Don't serve your work, but use your work to serve God and serve others.

WANT TO SEE THIS LIVED OUT?

Visit the Faith Driven Entrepreneur website at www.faithdrivenentrepreneur.org/book-stories to watch "Don't Worship Work," the story of Point B— a consulting firm that is breaking down the stereo- types of exhausted and overworked consultants by creating a healthy work-life balance for their entire company. Visit the URL to watch the full video and find thousands of other like-minded entrepreneurs going through the video study together.

CHAPTER 6

FAITH, FAMILY, WORK, AND FITNESS

Henry Kaestner

David Morken and I started Bandwidth because we wanted to solve a problem. We wanted to help companies get business internet connectivity effectively. At the time, there was this great mystery surrounding how to get good pricing, and businesses had a lot of questions about things like what T1 circuit they should get and who they should get it from. So we stepped in with the hopes of being the Expedia, Orbitz, or even today's KAYAK of business internet connectivity.

While Bandwidth has significantly broadened what it does over the years, it started with a mission to help. Now,

Bandwidth is a publicly traded company that provides tele-communications services to more than six thousand businesses including Google, Skype, Vonage, and Pinger. Our team started and then spun off Republic Wireless, a telco operator with a Wi-Fi enabled mobile service that was recently sold to DISH Network. And we got to create some super cool devices like the Relay (think of a cross between a walkie-talkie and a phone that is kid-friendly).

While the company has grown and experienced success, that's not what we hang our hats on at the end of the day. What gets us excited is that if you ask any of the more than one thousand employees who work at Bandwidth or Republic, they'll tell you that they love where they work. They say things like this:

- "Bandwidth has this energy that I think no other company has. Every day you come in here, you can just feel it."
- "I love the fact that it's very family oriented and a very relaxed environment."
- "The company has an amazing way of promoting you as an individual."

You don't get people to say those things by making a certain level of profit. The feelings that employees have for their workplace come from the values that drive the day-to-day work.

David and I wanted to see the same core values that drove our lives drive the company. We made sure that we, and all our employees, understood that Bandwidth was run for the glory of God and that its foundational principles are faith, family, work, and fitness—in that order. We defined success by our ability to balance all four values well.

In this chapter, we'll look at why those four principles created a healthy culture, and we'll use Bandwidth as a case study to show how to instill this in your own work as well as what to do when sticking to values gets hard.

Faith

The faith component is a given. Hopefully, the importance of founding your life and your work on a saving faith in Jesus Christ is clear at this point. But living that out isn't always as well-defined.

Paul reminds us in 1 Corinthians 13: "And now these three remain: faith, hope and love. But the greatest of these is love" (verse 13).

As Faith Driven Entrepreneurs, we knew the importance of faith. But when we were challenged on how to express it in our work, we knew we could always turn to love. Yes, you can share your testimony with your coworkers, talk openly about

> The way you live your life is often the greatest expression of faith and greatest form of evangelism you have.

attending church, and even invite others to join you. But the way you live your life is often the greatest expression of faith and greatest form of evangelism you have.

What am I doing today to love my employees? What am I doing today to love my customers? What am I doing today to love my shareholders? My partners? My vendors? The answers to these questions are the way we live out our faith. Love is an expression of faith. Why? Because of the reason behind our love: "We love because he first loved us" (1 John 4:19). If people want to know why we seek out chances to love, we can simply point them to Jesus. That's what our lives are about anyway, right?

Now, it's not easy to answer these questions and to act on love if you're relying solely on yourself. That's why the partnership between David and me, as well as our commitment to a local church body, was paramount to our expression of faith in the workplace. We've already talked about how the entrepreneurial journey isn't meant to be lived alone. But no journey in life is meant to be taken in isolation!

The people at our church were so encouraging and edifying both to me and David, as well as to any of our employees who came to find out what this faith thing was all about. If you've read this far, you know the importance of faith. And if you know why your faith matters, you know that you need a local community to keep you steadfast.

So, faith was one of our core values, definitely. But it expressed itself in love and local community.

Family

Just like with faith, David and I had a verse that we turned to whenever we needed reminding of the importance of family:

> Submit to one another out of reverence for Christ. Wives, submit yourselves to your own husbands as you do to the Lord. . . . Husbands, love your wives, just as Christ loved the church and gave himself up for her.
>
> EPHESIANS 5:21-22, 25

This is a challenging passage no matter which way you slice it. Husband, wife, man, woman. The command is hard. "Submit to one another"—give yourself up.

And let's be honest, few people are worse at this than entrepreneurs. We want what we want, and we do what it takes to get it. Plain and simple. If we have to work seventy hours this week to make sure the job gets done, then we will. But if we're failing to give Christlike love to our spouses in order to chase our businesses, we're missing out on one of God's toughest commands *and* one of his biggest blessings.

Entrepreneurs may wish this verse said, "Submit to your

work," but it just doesn't. The truth is that if you've committed to marriage, you've committed to a life of submission. Your job is to serve your spouse—an act that serves and glorifies God in itself.

So, how do we serve our spouses and still maintain our businesses? We instill a culture that says there are no heroics in staying late at the expense of family.

David and I made a practice of prioritizing one night a week that was dedicated to date night. We got babysitters and spent the evening loving and affirming our spouses. It wasn't just a great relational decision; it was a constant reminder of why we wanted to work so hard. We love our spouses and families and strive for excellence as a means of serving and providing for them.

If you are married, I recommend setting aside a date night with your spouse. Aside from date night, if you have children, make putting them to bed at night a priority. If the work still needs to get done, get back online once the kids have gone to bed. But before you go back, tell your spouse how grateful you are for their sacrifice in letting you build a business and grow a venture that you love.

Making family a priority in the fast-paced environment of an entrepreneur isn't going to happen naturally.

Making family a priority in the fast-paced environment of an entrepreneur isn't going to happen naturally. In fact, submitting to someone else is probably the least natural thing a person can do. But when we partner with our spouse—when we view them as an aid to our work, not as an obstacle—we get to experience the closest thing we can find to Christlike love this side of heaven.

Work

I love work. I think all entrepreneurs might say that. We love what we do. We like to lead, create, and innovate. We like to compete, and we like to win. We like to challenge those who work with us, just as they challenge us. We like to question, and we like to listen. We know we can always be better, and we love that, too. Work is the manifestation of so much of who we are and what we do. To paraphrase the famous line from *Chariots of Fire*, when we work, we feel God's pleasure.

That's why it always surprises me that when it comes to entrepreneurs defining personal values that flow into our businesses, it's easy to miss this one—work. This is especially surprising if we're looking to the Bible to inform our values. Jesus spent a lot of his time on earth teaching soft skills—love, kindness, forgiveness, and so on. But that doesn't mean he ignored work. The apostle Paul writes,

> Let the peace of Christ rule in your hearts, since
> as members of one body you were called to peace.
> And be thankful. Let the message of Christ dwell

among you richly as you teach and admonish
one another with all wisdom through psalms,
hymns, and songs from the Spirit, singing to God
with gratitude in your hearts. *And whatever you
do, whether in word or deed, do it all in the name
of the Lord Jesus, giving thanks to God the Father
through him.*

COLOSSIANS 3:15-17, EMPHASIS ADDED

We often read passages like this one from Colossians and
see the first half of it. Be peaceful. Be thankful. Sing with gratitude. Those are all great things, but it doesn't stop there. God
can't be confined to one part of our lives. He's not asking us to
worship him from nine to noon on Sunday mornings before
sending us out to do whatever we want during the week.

God belongs in our entrepreneurial journey. And that's
why work—specifically, diligent and faithful work—is
Bandwidth's third most important value. Don't leave God
in the church-sized box that many of us create for him, only
to be opened on Sundays. He should be in every meeting,
phone call, pitch, and presentation we have during the day.
In 1 Thessalonians 5:17, Paul writes that we should "pray
without ceasing" (ESV). These constant prayers are a consistent way to invite God into what we're doing. He's already
there, of course. But prayer allows us to open ourselves up to
receive and feel his presence.

In addition to honoring God by showing peace, gratitude, and thankfulness, we can also honor him in our diligence, perseverance, and faithfulness.

As Faith Driven Entrepreneurs, we don't get to be our own bosses. We have a higher calling—a higher authority to whom we report. If we must do everything in the name of the Lord Jesus, then it's best we do those things well.

Fitness

Work hard, play hard. *Mens sana in corpore sano.* ("A healthy mind in a healthy body.") Just about any cliché works here, and they all function in an effective faith-driven organization.

But why? What makes fitness such a high priority? We turn, once again, to the words of Scripture:

> Do you not know that your bodies are temples of the Holy Spirit, who is in you, whom you have received from God? You are not your own; you were bought at a price. Therefore honor God with your bodies.
>
> I CORINTHIANS 6:19-20

A main reason to encourage fitness in your company is because our bodies are a part of who we are, and God loves who we are. There's a reason God made humans with arms and legs and torsos and all the muscles and sinews that hold those things together. We are his creation, and it's our responsibility to honor what God has made. When we take care of ourselves, we show the one who made us that we care about who he is and what he has created. But beyond this, there are many practical benefits to placing an emphasis on fitness.

For starters, fitness provides an incredible opportunity for camaraderie. Whether running and biking together, or playing a game of ultimate frisbee during lunch, exercise offers a chance to rest from work and exchange ideas. There's a reason Googleplex has a beach volleyball court and Facebook HQ has a basketball court. Fitness is a great way to build a community and a culture.

At Bandwidth, when we would compete with team members from different departments, we experienced new levels of empathy and understanding. We were training ourselves to appreciate other people's jobs. Engineers, salespeople, and the finance department got to see one another outside of their roles at work. And in doing so, we became a better team in and out of the office.

Not to mention the idea that corporate fitness can be downright fun. We have won the citywide ice hockey championship, entered a team in the TransRockies mountain bike race and finished second, and even entered a team in the Race Across America (RAAM) and won it!

Improved fitness leads to improved productivity. A

Harvard study showed that regular exercise can enhance creativity, quicken learning, sharpen memory, and improve concentration.[3] And that's great, but the intangible benefits of increased camaraderie, empathy, and a shared competitive spirit can't be understated and make fitness a worthy value to incorporate.

>

Anyone can lay out core values for their company. Defining what your business is all about is a great start, but that's exactly what it is—a start. Inevitably, there will come a time when these values get put to the test. At Bandwidth, this happened early.

In our first year of business, we had twenty-five employees and $74,000 in revenue. I'm not sure if you caught it, but that math doesn't lend itself to sustainability. In the second full year, we had thirty employees and $264,000 in revenue. Better, but we were still so far away from sustainability that it was difficult to see a real future for the company.

David and I were rapidly running out of the money that we had earned from previous ventures and invested into Bandwidth. We were strapped, to say the least. Things were getting desperate.

Right in the middle of this time, an incredible deal came to the company. The deal was for us to provide an

OC3 circuit, which in internet parlance is a very big internet pipe. Closing this deal would result in a huge payday, thus extending the life of the business that seemed near its end.

We had—and still have—one big rule in dealing with new customers: they couldn't be from the adult entertainment business, which is by far the largest relative consumer of internet access of any industry. If we had been able to do business with them, we would have had far less financial stress in our early days. But our values kept us from associating with them. For us, the adult entertainment industry stood against both our faith and our family values, so we weren't going anywhere near it.

At any rate, the company buying the OC3 looked clean. The sales rep checked them out, and they passed muster. We were on our way to turning the financial corner. We closed the deal. There were lots of high fives. And then the problem came.

In provisioning the circuit, we came to find that the corporation that bought the circuit was merely a holding company for other companies in—you guessed it—the adult entertainment business.

The big dilemma for us wasn't whether we would provision the circuit and get the payday—we knew our values wouldn't allow that. But should we pay the sales rep a commission for a deal that ultimately never materialized?

We had never had to face that before. We ultimately

canceled the deal with the company, and we determined that the rep had done the requisite amount of diligence on the deal and paid him his commission. At a time when our cash balance had never been lower, we paid the highest commission check we had ever paid.

But it was also the very point from which our company turned around. Seeing our business brought to the brink and how everyone was willing to stay committed to our values gave us the energy we needed to keep going. We knew we were on to something. And we weren't wrong. From 2003 to 2007 we were the fourth-fastest-growing privately held company in the country—growth that we achieved without significant outside funding or by making acquisitions.

Now, I know that's not how every story ends. There's no promise that sticking to your values will inevitably lead to success. But the inward reward of faithfulness far outweighs any possible outward reward.

> **When we live lives of integrity, we are living out the calling God has placed on our lives.**

Integrity comes from aligning our thoughts, words, and actions. And when we live lives of integrity—keeping our inner principles in line with our outward actions—we are living out the calling God has placed on our lives. That is especially so when we lead our businesses with integrity.

That's what being a Faith Driven Entrepreneur is all about.

WANT TO SEE THIS LIVED OUT?

Visit the Faith Driven Entrepreneur website at www.faithdrivenentrepreneur.org/book-stories to watch Henry Kaestner and David Morken, cofounders of Bandwidth, describe their four company values. Visit the URL to watch the full video and find thousands of other like-minded entrepreneurs going through the video study together.

CHAPTER 7

EXCELLENCE MATTERS

Henry Kaestner

If you walk into your local American bookstore, past the bestsellers and new fiction, you'll find a section for Christian fiction. I've often wondered why Christianity gets its own genre of novels. There's no section for Jewish or Muslim fiction, yet our religion has its own marketplace—set apart from the general fiction you can find anywhere else in the store.

The Christian-specific market for Christian-specific products isn't a problem in and of itself. I've read great Christian books. I've bought great products from Christian businesses that were selling Christian-specific products. But having a separate market does create the potential for exploitation.

A market-savvy person can recognize that Christians

represent a lot of buying power. If you can make a product tailored to their wants and preferences, you've got a profitable business on your hands. The problem is that this creates the opportunity for exploitation, and we'd rather see the Christian market be defined by excellence. Unfortunately, second-rate work has often become the norm, and in many circles, "Christian" is associated with poor quality.

Again, there's nothing wrong with creating something specifically for Christians. The issue arises when the Christian label becomes an excuse for less than stellar work.

My day-to-day life is now focused on investing, and there are plenty of people in my circle who are reluctant to invest in "Christian funds." Why? Because they associate "Christian" with "second-rate." Of course, I've seen Christian funds that consistently outperform secular funds, but there's still a negative connotation because of a lack of excellence in some areas of the marketplace. My heart hurts for the faithful men and women doing incredible work who aren't getting the time of day from investors because others have spoiled the Christian name with shoddy workmanship.

This is why excellence matters. Faith Driven Entrepreneurs represent more than just themselves and their businesses— they represent the God they worship. We reflect the faith community we've aligned with. It's this very idea that should propel us to go above and beyond when it comes to the quality of our work.

We believe that we were created in the image of a God who worked six days out of seven and whose work was *good*. Praise God he didn't cut corners when creating the plants and animals! What makes us think that we should be any different?

> Faith Driven Entrepreneurs represent more than just themselves and their businesses—they represent the God they worship.

>

I once heard this quote from Jim Carrey that has always stuck with me: "I think everybody should get rich and famous and do everything they ever dreamed of so they can see that it's not the answer."

Talk about a bleak idea! You mean to tell me that at the end of this mountain climb, once I obtain the status and success I'm constantly striving for, it won't be enough? Hitting my financial targets, receiving the recognition I deserve, making the blockbuster sale won't satisfy me?

I think Jim Carrey is hitting at something profound here. Selfish accomplishments never satisfy. Hitting my goals, building my business, receiving my recognition won't do it. There's an emptiness in pursuing excellence purely for excellence's sake. When we're trying our best to boost our own self-esteem, we'll eventually find that our best isn't enough. Then, the results and the process of obtaining them become a burden.

When we're excellent for God, by contrast, we find joy in

the process. That's been my experience as long as I've been an entrepreneur and investor. I find joy, not always in the sheer energy required to work hard, but in the knowledge that my efforts serve a higher purpose than my own. And if we're honest with ourselves, I think we'll realize that while meeting our goals is great, there's only so much happiness that we can bring ourselves. Serving ourselves is a dead end, no matter how good we are at it.

But Faith Driven Entrepreneurs have a different approach. We set goals, take action, and work through an efficient process to meet set standards. But none of that requires our best *until* we put God in his rightful place. He's both our reason for starting *and* our motivation for finishing well.

I am not the light at the end of my own tunnel. A luxurious retirement plan isn't my goal. My goal, as a believer, is to stand before God at the end of my life, knowing that I've placed my very best sacrifice at his feet, knowing that I will hear, "Well done, my good and faithful servant."

The idea of standing before God and presenting what you have done can either terrify you or inspire you. If the former, remember that God is shown to be a Father running to meet his wayward son. He's excited to welcome you to your eternal home, to reward you for a job well done. We can be elated to go out every day and do great work for the glory of God, knowing that we don't have to earn his approval. He is a God worth working for.

If you're still not convinced, let me ask you this: If the god you worship isn't worthy of your best, then how weak is your god?

My God is full of joy and life and grace and mercy and excellence and faithfulness and beauty and wonder and so much more. An awareness of who God is makes me want to do nothing less than serve him with every waking minute of my life.

Are there days when the work is hard and I don't want to do it? Of course. I'm a human. I'm sinful, and I fall short of this standard again and again and again. I can't achieve excellence for myself day after day. I just can't.

But I can do it for God. When I'm in tune with what God has called me to do, I can't see a better way of living and working than living and working for God.

>

Francis Schaeffer once taught that it's the degree to which we do our work well that we have an opportunity to witness and be heard. Think about that for a second.

For someone, you may be the closest they get to Jesus. You might interact with customers who will never step foot in a church their entire life. They're looking at you and seeing the image of God. What does that image look like?

It's for this reason that Faith Driven Entrepreneurs shouldn't just meet the standard of excellence the market demands. They should exceed it. We aren't creating products and providing services solely for our customers. We report to a higher authority. As Colossians says, "Whatever you do, work at it with all your heart, as working for the Lord, not for human masters" (3:23).

If we're working for the Lord, then excellence is the base expectation. Excellence is the bare minimum. There's no room for cutting corners, for settling for less than our best, because the God we worship never did.

> **If we're working for the Lord, then excellence is the base expectation. Excellence is the bare minimum.**

It's hard to imagine wobbly chairs coming out of the carpentry shop in Nazareth. I don't see Jesus slapping an ichthus fish on the bottom of passable tables and selling them to anyone. Everything in his life reflected God. That means his craftsmanship was perfect.

Praise God that expectation isn't placed upon us—our lack of perfection is the reason for our faith in Jesus. But also praise God that he gives us the chance to strive toward some form of excellence this side of heaven.

That's what you get to do every day. You get to wake up and think, *How can I best reflect the image of God to the unbelieving world?* Part of the answer to that question is doing a great job.

Look at how perfect this is when it comes full circle.

Reflecting the image of a perfect God demands excellence, but that same God has already achieved perfection so that we don't have to. We then get to achieve excellence without the pressure of having to achieve perfection. Instead, we get to live and work out of a deep gratitude for who God is and a daily dependence on his finished work at the Cross.

It's hard not to get emotional thinking about that. Our God is amazing, and the fact that we *get* to give our best to him every day is an absolute gift. Even better is the fact that he can take our efforts and turn them into a witness for his character.

Because when we're excited to work hard, we stand out. When we're working hard to do excellent work without the added pressure of needing some sort of perfection, we look different from the world. And people will want to know where that comes from.

>

The simple truth is this: God asks for our best work—not what our culture has come to define as the best "Christian version" of our work.

Christianity should be synonymous with excellence for two reasons. One, we reflect the image of a perfect (not merely excellent) God. He has raised us up to the standard of perfection by sending Christ to live and die in our place, and we get to live in that freedom every day. Working hard and achieving excellence is a privilege.

And two, our perfect God can use our work to share his love with an unbelieving world. When people interact with us, our services, and our products, there's the possibility that they will notice something different, something that sets us apart. And we get to point them to God when that happens.

We're not doing great work to receive the glory, nor are we trying hard to achieve perfection on this side of heaven. We're working hard because there is great joy in giving our best to the God who has already given his best on our behalf.

WANT TO SEE THIS LIVED OUT?

Visit the Faith Driven Entrepreneur website at www.faithdrivenentrepreneur.org/book-stories to watch Don Flow, CEO of Flow Automotive, describe why excellence is important to his business. Visit the URL to watch the full video and find thousands of other like-minded entrepreneurs going through the video study together.

CHAPTER 8

FAITHFUL VS. WILLFUL

Chip Ingram

I remember talking one day with a venture capitalist who had been overwhelmingly successful in Silicon Valley. We're talking about someone who was in on the ground floor of companies such as Google, Amazon, and Facebook.

He was alongside the founders of these enterprises as they processed their dreams and visions, he joined their launches, and he helped facilitate the growth of their businesses. This led me to ask him one day, "What do you look for in an entrepreneur?"

We both knew that the majority of start-ups fail, yet he had been a part of several incredibly successful companies.

As we sat in a coffee shop, I asked him that question, and he talked about how fortunate he was and went on about how blessed he felt to have been involved. And I said, "Look, I get all that. But it wasn't just blind fortune. What are you looking for in entrepreneurs and businesses that come through your door?"

He responded with a list of six or seven things, but three stood out to me:

- a sense of urgency
- a conviction that their idea will work
- a bias for action

Each of those makes total sense. Entrepreneurs are the type of people who want to make things happen *now*. Urgency is clearly in the DNA of some of the most successful men and women.

Conviction is the same. You can imagine the founders of Google sitting with the idea that they were going to make all the information in the world instantly available to everyone in the world. That's incredibly ambitious, but they had a deep personal conviction that it was actually possible and that they could make it happen.

Then, bias for action. Great entrepreneurs don't whine and complain when faced with difficulties and obstacles. Instead, they act. They even view failure as an opportunity to learn, to grow, to adjust. You hear entrepreneurs constantly working with the idea that this has to happen. Let's get moving. Let's keep going. They fight through every barrier, every mountain, every challenge, every funding issue.

Think about these character traits in terms of Christian entrepreneurs, and suddenly the stakes are even higher. Rather than "I need to make this happen," it's "I need to make this happen *because God told me to*." In other words, "God gave me this idea. God spoke to me about starting this company. God wants me to use this platform and money and influence for his Kingdom. I'm all in. I'm totally committed. This is God's business. I'm going to do this for him, and I'm going to impact people for good."

That's another plane that Faith Driven Entrepreneurs operate on. And that's where we find the tension between faithfulness and willfulness. What we, especially as entrepreneurs, often fail to realize is that we can be 100 percent committed to God's will and God's purpose while actually trying to do God's will through our own strength, our own power, and out of our own resources. We can be 100 percent committed to God's will and 100 percent certain we can bring it about ourselves.

The three traits that this investor described as ideal characteristics for a successful entrepreneur are the same

> **God's will being done through *our* urgency, *our* conviction, and *our* power isn't God's will at all.**

things that can lead us astray as Christians. Because God's will being done through *our* urgency, *our* conviction, and *our* power isn't God's will at all.

Willfulness—the "I will make this happen no matter what" mentality—despite its sincerity, is not God's way. It leaves many entrepreneurs discouraged, frustrated, tired, burned out, and disillusioned after seeking to build or start or grow a business for God's glory. The good news is we're not alone. The disciples did exactly the same thing.

>

Let's set the scene. The disciples were all in. Jesus had called them to follow him, and they had left their families and their businesses to do just that. They were committed to Christ. They were following him, performing miracles in his name, and spreading the name of Jesus rapidly from town to town.

Then we get to Mark 8, where Jesus feeds the four thousand. This is a familiar story, but we're going to look at what happens right after Jesus feeds everyone. He and the disciples are in a boat leaving the area, and the disciples realize they've forgotten to bring bread. (Remember, they have *just* watched Jesus feed thousands of people with almost nothing!) Jesus tells them, metaphorically, to beware the Pharisees' leaven, and the disciples instantly misunderstand him by focusing on the bread they've forgotten. To which

Jesus responds, "Why are you talking about having no bread? Do you still not see or understand? Are your hearts hardened? Do you have eyes but fail to see, and ears but fail to hear?" (Mark 8:17-18).

Are your hearts hardened? Can you imagine hearing that as a disciple? They've left their families, their businesses, their way of life to follow this guy they've just met. They've watched him do incredible things, heard him proclaimed the Son of God. They're completely committed to him.

And Jesus says they have hard hearts? Why?

Because they're focused on *their* way, *their* efforts, and *their* work, not the work of God among them. They're focused on the bread they don't have—as if a lack of bread has ever stopped Jesus!

The story of Jesus feeding four thousand and the boat ride afterward bring up a fundamental issue that every entrepreneur has to deal with: Who is going to be your resource? You will never have enough money. You will never have enough staff. You will never have enough opportunity. Here we see Jesus teach the disciples that *he's* the resource.

When the crowd was hungry, Jesus told the disciples, "You feed them." That's what God does. He asks us to do the impossible with what we don't have. Think about that.

God expects us to do the impossible with what we don't have, because that paradigm means we have to trust him. The disciples mistakenly thought God's number-one priority was accomplishing something great for the Kingdom. What Jesus showed them was that he had to work in them deeply before he was going to work through them significantly. That's just as true for us.

As entrepreneurs, we can get so excited about the idea, the business, the growth, the impact—whatever it is—that we forget that God's number-one priority is not the project. His number-one priority is growing our faith and making us more like his Son.

In John 6, another story of Jesus' miraculous feeding, the people ask Jesus, "What must we do to do the works God requires?" They're asking, "What does God want me to do? How does God want me to work?" And Jesus' response is simple: "The work of God is this: to believe in the one he has sent" (verses 28-29).

That's God's endgame. It's not your growth, your business, your profit, your loss, your anything. It's that all would trust in him. Faithfulness is following this mission—doing our part but leaving the results to God. Willfulness is making sure the mission gets accomplished in our way, on our timeline, through our efforts.

We must come to the point where God is our resource, where God is our provider. It's God's plan, and we will help accomplish his purpose—in his way, in his time, and through his methods.

As entrepreneurs, when we try to willfully make God's plan happen—when we try to feed thousands with a handful of measly loaves—we fail. Our identity gets wrapped up in our own efforts. Our reputation or value is wrapped up in our ability, or lack thereof, to make our business venture a success.

Of course, we're *Faith Driven* Entrepreneurs, so "for God's glory" becomes our mantra, but in willfulness, our priorities are completely misplaced. We work harder and longer. We experience burnout, discouragement, anxiety, fear, and anger because we try to accomplish "God's will" our way.

Jesus knew the disciples couldn't feed all those people. God knows we can't do it all. What he really wants is for us to look to him and say, "I can't do it. You can. Help me."

That posture is so different, right? We typically don't imagine entrepreneurs asking for help. We're supposed to be the ones who have the answers, who "make it happen." Often I've fallen into the trap of thinking I had to go it alone. I've experienced burnout from misplaced priorities that came close to destroying my health and the most important relationship in my life.

But this posture of helplessness, strangely, lets me breathe a sigh of relief. I want to do it all—I want to be a bastion of strength and success—but deep down I know I can't, and deep down I want someone else to be the strong one. Don't you feel that a little bit? Aren't you at least a little exhausted from being the one everyone relies on? Aren't you tired of your efforts being the only thing keeping your business, your marriage, your family afloat? It doesn't have to be that way.

Fighting to accomplish God's will on our own isn't faithfulness. It's masochism. But we all do it. We've all told our spouses that "it's just for a season—I just need to push through this, work really hard for a few months, then everything will slow down." No, it won't. Our drivenness must give way to dependency. Trying harder and harder on our own steam will ultimately result in the neglect of God, our family, our friends, and our health. Trust has to replace this attitude.

>

I have a good buddy, a business guy who used to run Kentucky Fried Chicken. And he once told me something that has always stuck with me. He said for years when he got really committed to Christ, he would meet with God in the morning during his quiet time and would feel like God was saying, "Okay, we've met now. Go get 'em, champ." And he would go about his day, leaving God at home while he worked.

I think we've all had those seasons when we meet with God in the morning just to check a box, then we go out and do whatever it is we think God has sent us to do on our own. In reality, what God wants is to work with us. The message isn't "Go get 'em." It's "Let's do this together."

It's the difference between working *for* God's approval and working *from* God's approval. We don't go out to earn our way back into God's good graces. We go out already in God's good graces, working with him as he works through us.

My KFC friend now says that when he meets with God in the morning, he realizes that God already knows his dreams and his desires. And now he feels God putting his arm around him and saying, "Okay, let's go get 'em, champ." In other words, every meeting, every decision, isn't detached from a sectioned-off time we spend with God. It's all infused with God's presence because he's always with us.

That's faithfulness. It doesn't mean we don't work hard. We still get up early, still work hard, still innovate. We refuse to let barriers deter us. But it's no longer us working for God. It's us joining him and working with one eye on the project and one eye on the bigger priority of what he wants to do in us and in the people around us, first and foremost.

It means being able to wait on his timing and his provision as we release all the pressure to be successful, to make it happen, to do it on our own, to pit our reputation and glory against God's.

The challenge then lies not in our outward behavior but in our inward heart posture. Faithfulness and willfulness look a lot alike to anyone passing by. It's just like the two houses Jesus describes in Matthew 7. One is built on rock and one is built on sand. They both require energy, effort, passion, and innovation, and both entail setbacks and breakthroughs. But internally, they're worlds apart.

To clarify, willfulness vs. faithfulness looks something like this:

	Willfulness	Faithfulness
Perspective	I have to make this happen.	I will work hard, but only God can make it happen.
Work	There's no room for anything but this. I'm obsessed and preoccupied.	This is important but not consuming. It isn't my life. It's just a part of my life.
Emotions	I feel anxious, stressed, and under pressure.	I feel calm, confident, and at peace.
Responsibility	I own the outcomes. I have to achieve this.	God owns the outcomes, not me. I'm faithful to trust, work hard, wait, and risk. But the outcomes don't belong to me.

In short, willfulness is about striving, performing, and achieving to prove our worth. By contrast, faithfulness is about contending, trusting, and pursuing obedience characterized by personal holiness in relational dependency to fulfill God's purposes.

We all want to be in that "Faithfulness" column. So, how do we do it? We follow the example God gave us. Jesus modeled four things that can help us move from the willfulness column into a life of faithfulness and the joy that follows.

Authentic Humility

I have set you an example that you should do as I have done for you.

JOHN 13:15

Jesus said this to his disciples after he had taken the posture of a servant and washed their feet. Jesus modeled humility in every aspect of his ministry. He valued others above himself. He sought out those in need, and he met those needs.

Willful entrepreneurs create businesses that revolve around them—their talents, their drive, their energy, their vision. Faithful entrepreneurs understand that life isn't about them, and neither is their business.

Eternal Perspective

If I go and prepare a place for you, I will come back
and take you to be with me that you also may be
where I am.

JOHN 14:3

Jesus' ministry always had his death, resurrection, and return in mind. He moved toward the eternal mission God called him to. He healed and fed people along the way, but he never lost sight of what God had called him to do—bring eternal life to all who believe.

Willful entrepreneurs are constantly trying to pull an unpredictable future into the present, always trying to wrestle the unknown under their control. Faithful entrepreneurs already know the end of the story—that God wins and that they will one day live with him in eternity. They work hard with that in mind, knowing that the outcome has already been decided by God and that their role is to enjoy the process of achieving it alongside him.

Abiding Attitude

Remain in me, as I also remain in you. No branch
can bear fruit by itself; it must remain in the vine.
Neither can you bear fruit unless you remain
in me.

JOHN 15:4

Jesus stayed connected to his Father at all times. We see him going away to be alone, to pray, to commune with his Father in heaven. If Jesus took the time and made the effort to abide in his Father, how much more do we need to focus on abiding in our Father?

Willful entrepreneurs can't sit still long enough to be with God. They always have to be going, running, working, making things happen, striving to keep the mission and the business from falling apart. Faithful entrepreneurs work hard but know that working apart from a connection with God is pointless. They're aware of what it means to abide, and they're tuned in to knowing when they need to unplug from work and slow down in order to commune with God.

Realistic Expectations

> I have told you these things, so that in me you may have peace. In this world you will have trouble. But take heart! I have overcome the world.
>
> JOHN 16:33

Jesus knew exactly what was going to happen, and he didn't try to hide the truth from his disciples. He knew the brutal death that awaited him, yet he still willingly walked into it so that we might be saved.

Willful entrepreneurs believe that the outcomes are

> **Faithful entrepreneurs expect God to never leave or forsake them, and that promise alone is enough to get them through any setback or difficulty.**

under their control. Therefore, they do everything they can to manipulate things to their liking, hoping that they can create an end that fits with their desires. Faithful entrepreneurs know that the outcomes belong to God, so they don't get distracted worrying about how things will end. They expect God to remain faithful to them and to never leave or forsake them, and that promise alone is enough to get them through any setback or difficulty.

>

I wish I could tell you there's a switch you can flip to go from willful to faithful, but there isn't. It's an ongoing and intentional process and a lifelong journey—one that you won't get right every day. But you can know with absolute certainty that you matter more to Christ than anything you can accomplish or achieve. His desires for you are great, but his expectations are patient and reasonable. Seek first his Kingdom and his righteousness every day in every way, as Jesus commanded, and you will be greeted each and every morning by a God who looks at you and says, "You are my child, unconditionally loved, equipped to change the world as you work alongside me. Bring me your loaves and your fish, and let's do this together."

WANT TO SEE THIS LIVED OUT?

Visit the Faith Driven Entrepreneur website at www.faithdrivenentrepreneur.org/book-stories to watch "God Loves Cabinets," the story of Steve Bell and Bellmont Cabinets. Visit the URL to watch the full video and find thousands of other like-minded entre-preneurs going through the video study together.

CHAPTER 9

MINISTRY IN DEED

Henry Kaestner

When I was at Bandwidth, we had a general manager who thought that having a corporate chaplain was a terrible idea. He said, "Look, I know you guys are Christians, I know you care about your faith. That's cool. But a chaplain walking around will make it feel like a church here. It won't feel like a business."

We listened to that feedback, thought it over, and prayed about it, but we decided to hire a part-time chaplain anyway. We really believed that having a chaplain available to our employees was important. We explained to everyone that the chaplain was there to meet with them, get coffee, take them to lunch, and talk about whatever they wanted to talk about. His position was a specific line item in our budget so that everyone would feel cared for. That was it.

We didn't encourage anyone to talk to him about faith or God, or even anything serious. We just presented him as a resource.

The first three months of having a chaplain were a little awkward. He would walk around the office fairly regularly, chatting with people, checking in, saying hello. But then, four months in, the daughter of one of our managers was in a bad car accident. The chaplain visited the family at the hospital and stayed with them for the next forty-eight hours.

Six months after that, one of our employees employees died during the workday. Again, the chaplain was a huge source of relief for that employee's family and was able to provide an immense blessing to our other employees just by being there. That's when people realized they could talk to him.

Suddenly his plate was full, and the same general manager who had been against hiring a chaplain in the first place came to us and asked if we could bring on a second chaplain. So, we did.

When I think about that story, I'm so grateful for the ways in which leading a business provides tangible ways to express God's love to our partners, customers, employees, and vendors alike.

For our employees, we get to show them love by giving

them meaningful work and leading them well. We get to offer competitive salaries and create space for them to lead and love their families. A well-loved employee is then in a great spot to love the customer. For example, few companies do a better job of delighting their customers than Chick-fil-A. Why are their drive-thru attendants so kind, patient, and attentive? It's not because Chick-fil-A headquarters has outlined these characteristics as core virtues. It's because they are constantly trying to think how they might make their employees' jobs better by engineering out the aspects of their work that cause frustration.

In the same way that this attitude toward others can trickle down through our employees and to our customers, our vendors and partners can experience that type of care. That's what ministry in deed is all about. It's a chance to view every work-based relationship as a chance to physically display the virtues God is instilling in us.

Ministry in deed is part of our calling as Christians. There are many ways that we can do this, but for the Faith Driven Entrepreneur, I want to highlight a few that might not come immediately to mind. We can minister well by being honest with ourselves and with others, leading from a place of brokenness, and setting a vision that others want to follow.

>

David is a pretty epic biblical character. We know that he killed lions and bears, defeated Goliath, had a dominant military career, and on top of everything else, that God referred to him as "a man after [God's] own heart" (Acts 13:22). It seems like he pretty much had it all together.

But if we read some of what David wrote in Psalms, his life sounds terrible. He talks about being lonely and afflicted, being in anguish, and even feeling like he's drowning. "I will fear no evil, for you are with me" and "My God, my God, why have you forsaken me?" were both written by David—in back-to-back Psalms (23 and 22). How is that even possible?

> With high highs usually come low lows. This is the nature of being an entrepreneur. In fact, these highs and lows are often separated by a matter of hours.

It's a cruel irony that we often assume the people who experience the most success usually endure the least amount of suffering. In the story of David, as well as the story of many entrepreneurs, the opposite is true. With high highs usually come low lows. This is the nature of being an entrepreneur. In fact, these highs and lows are often separated by a matter of hours.

But here's a profound lesson we can learn from David's life: he didn't hide his emotions. When he was happy and having a great day, he let God know. And when he was miserable and depressed, he let God know that, too. In all things, he told God what was going on in his heart and mind.

It's all too easy to talk about God when things are going great. We wear our faith on our sleeves when we've spent a great morning in prayer. But what about the days and weeks when our faith feels dry, or when God seems silent?

David gives us such a great example of what it's like to be totally honest. God doesn't change, but we experience him through the lens of our lives, which is a constant roller-coaster ride—especially for entrepreneurs.

Yet for Christians, there's a big misconception that being an example of Christ to others means having it all together and being happy all the time, or at least appearing that way. That's just not the example I see in the Bible. And this makes sense, because in my experience, Christians *don't* have it all together, and people have a pretty good lie detector. They can intuitively feel whether they trust somebody, whether another person really cares about them, or whether their interaction is just part of a transaction.

But when we're honest—both with ourselves and with others—we invite people to see a real relationship with God. My relationship with God isn't perfect—because while God is perfect, I am not. But that's okay.

In fact, my own weaknesses, as Paul says, are my exact reason to boast. We can minister to others by living lives of integrity. That means I don't have to sugarcoat my life when things aren't going well. I can acknowledge the reality around me and still say, "I don't totally understand what's going on, but I trust God." What a powerful witness that is!

As an entrepreneur, you already feel the pressures of needing to succeed and have it all together. But you can realize that not having it all together is exactly what God will use to draw people closer to you and closer to him. By being honest with yourself and others, you can minister to others, inviting them into a similar place of honesty where they can meet God.

>

We all want to appear like we have it all together. As entrepreneurs, we want our investors, employees, and customers to know that everything is under control. We can take care of everything. We can handle whatever comes our way.

The problem with this attitude is that it often involves our putting up a front. Trying to manipulate the way others perceive us is a slippery slope because eventually all we have is the false frame that others see with no concept of our actual self that lies within it. We can quickly become walking shells of humans with personalities we've merely created for ourselves.

But in Luke 18, Jesus paints an incredible picture of the difference between someone who manages their image and someone who is honest about who they are:

To some who were confident of their own righteousness and looked down on everyone else, Jesus told this parable: "Two men went up to the temple to pray, one a Pharisee and the other a tax collector. The Pharisee stood by himself and prayed: 'God, I thank you that I am not like other people—robbers, evildoers, adulterers—or even like this tax collector. I fast twice a week and give a tenth of all I get.'

"But the tax collector stood at a distance. He would not even look up to heaven, but beat his breast and said, 'God, have mercy on me, a sinner.'

"I tell you that this man, rather than the other, went home justified before God. For all those who exalt themselves will be humbled, and those who humble themselves will be exalted."

LUKE 18:9-14

In this parable, we see the Pharisee trying to persuade God to perceive him in a certain light. He keeps the things he's ashamed of to himself and comes to God with only the good—his fasting and tithing.

But for the tax collector, there's no front. He knows that he's a sinner, and he knows that God knows, so why try to hide it? All he asks for is mercy. He doesn't try to curry favor, doesn't try to bring blessing upon himself. He just wants grace. And as Jesus explains, it's this heart posture of humility that leads to the man's justification.

Entrepreneurs can very easily act like the Pharisee in this parable. We can present information—to our shareholders, our friends, our families—that serves as a means of self-justification. "I'm going to meet our next quarter goals." "I'm

> When we stop
> pretending like we
> have everything
> under control and
> start showing others
> the truth, our lives
> become a walking
> witness to the God
> we worship.

going to make sure the job gets done." "I'm going to be everywhere people need me to be."

But here's the truth: we can't do it alone, and even if we could, it's not about us anyway. God wants our honest hearts, not the facades we put up for others or the version of ourselves we're most proud of. But to give him our honest hearts requires humility. And the terrifying truth is that if we don't humble ourselves, God might do it for us. He has changed kings and altered kingdoms. If he needs to take away our business to remind us that he is God, that seems well within his reach.

When we stop pretending like we have everything under control and start showing others the truth, our lives become a walking witness to the God we worship. Why? Because even if the business is crumbling all around us, we can still point others to the eternal hope we have in Christ.

Ministering in deed isn't acting like we have all the answers. It's living our lives openly and honestly so that God can shine through our brokenness.

>

As leaders of businesses, entrepreneurs get to let everyone know where the team is going and the role they play in getting the team there. This sounds basic, and it is. But it's very hard to do well.

We need to paint a picture of what success looks like so that the end goal becomes real to those around us—so real they can almost taste it. Or as author Madeleine L'Engle writes, "We draw people to Christ not by loudly discrediting what they believe, by telling them how wrong they are and how right we are, but by showing them a light that is so lovely that they want with all their hearts to know the source of it."[4] Ministry in deed is the act of living a life that gives light to those who see you.

We talked about sharing our faith at work and what it looks like to praise God in every opportunity, but what we haven't addressed is that our very existence is an incredible opportunity to share God's love. The way we live can make the Good News of Jesus obvious and irresistible.

That means we're more than just the messengers of God's love. We're the models of his good works. We share the love of God, and we show it in the way we live.

Jesus did this, right? He didn't just preach and teach and talk about who God was. No, he showed it in the way he lived. He performed miracles, treated others kindly, and followed through on everything he had shared all the way up to dying for our sins. He modeled God's love.

If you want to know what it looks like to successfully

minister in deed, it means being the type of person who makes people stop and ask, "What makes them different?"

People who understand who God is and what he's done act differently than people who don't. There's a different peace, a different assurance, a different attitude that follows those who believe in Jesus.

People who model God's love are intention and integrity in action. They have an *actual* interest in others. They love their neighbor because they first care about their neighbor. That's who God has placed us on earth to be.

While talking about your faith at work is great, evangelism doesn't stop there. Sharing God's love with others means showing God's love to them in tangible ways that they can receive and understand. It means ministry in deed.

WANT TO SEE THIS LIVED OUT?

Visit the Faith Driven Entrepreneur website at www.faithdrivenentrepreneur.org/book-stories to watch "People Can," the story of Camcraft, a family-owned, precision-manufacturing company near Chicago with a mission "to glorify God," about the importance of caring for employees. Visit the URL to watch the full video and find thousands of other like-minded entrepreneurs going through the video study together.

CHAPTER 10

MINISTRY IN WORD

Henry Kaestner

Sharing our faith is important. Obviously. In his last words on earth, Jesus gave his followers what is now known as the great commission: "Go and make disciples of all nations, baptizing them in the name of the Father and of the Son and of the Holy Spirit, and teaching them to obey everything I have commanded you" (Matthew 28:19-20).

The question is, how? You may have heard a quote that is often misattributed to St. Francis of Assisi: "Preach the gospel at all times. When necessary, use words."

My struggle with this quote is that it creates an unnecessary hierarchy between preaching by our actions and preaching by our words. We could go back and forth on this forever, but why not both? The love of Christ can be seen in the way his followers live their lives, but we shouldn't stop there. Our words should absolutely back up our actions.

There are opportunities to "minister in word" everywhere. David knew this: "I will give you thanks in the great assembly; among the throngs I will praise you" (Psalm 35:18). Imagine what it would look like to praise God everywhere we went. This idea may conjure an image of someone walking around the office with their hands raised singing worship songs, but that's not what I'm suggesting.

I'm suggesting that every place and every person is an *opportunity* to share the good news of what Christ has done in our lives. This perspective changes the way we live. Think of how different your life might look if you sprinkled truth throughout every conversation you had during the day.

> Every single place you go and every single person you encounter is presenting you with an opportunity to praise God by living and loving in a way that draws others to him.

When we read these words of David, terms like "the great assembly" and "the throngs" probably don't sound familiar. But we still have those today; they just look different. We have an office space. We have coworkers gathered together for lunch. We have meetings with investors. We have conversations with customers. God can be praised in both our words and our actions in those moments.

Evangelism is a vocal activity, and every single place you go and every single person you encounter is presenting you with an opportunity to praise God by living and loving in a way that draws others to him. And if entrepreneurs are good at anything, it's seizing opportunities.

But if you feel nervous, uncertain, or awkward, I get it. That's why I want to walk you through how you can share your personal testimony, what it looks like to be winsome, and why prayer is the linchpin of your ministry.

>

Simon Sinek has a powerful TED Talk titled "How Great Leaders Inspire Action." In it, he talks about the importance of "why." He uses Apple, Martin Luther King Jr., and the Wright brothers as examples of what can happen when we are in touch with our core motivations for living and doing what we do.

He shares how almost everyone knows what they do, many people know how they do it, but few know or even acknowledge why they do it. He asks the audience to consider their purpose, their cause, their reason for existence.

In business, the "why" behind what you do is crucial. Entrepreneurs especially know this. You're not going to get out of bed every morning and enter the risky start-up world if you don't have a strong motivation for why you're doing this in the first place.

The same is true when it comes to integrating our faith and our work.

For many of us, "God's will" for our lives often remains mysteriously indiscernible, something we fear we may never quite understand or figure out. We all want to know what God's plan is for our lives. But asking about God's will isn't the right question. When we do this, we're focusing on the what instead of the why.

We can find some clarity in Proverbs: "Commit to the LORD whatever you do, and he will establish your plans" (16:3). Notice that this verse says to commit "whatever you do." It doesn't say "figure out exactly what God would have you do and then do *that* for his glory"—although that may be today's common wisdom when we talk about God's will. Rather, it says to commit *whatever you do* to God. That's your why.

The what of your business is less important than the why. And the why is so that God would be glorified in all of it.

Maybe it took you a long time to start your business because you weren't sure if doing so was God's will. Regardless of how you came to discern what God's will actually is, you can now live in the fact that God's will is for you to glorify him in whatever you do. Period.

And the way in which you got to where you are is a journey. It's your personal testimony. The life you've experienced, the ups and downs you've gone through, all testify to the way God has worked in your life. If you feel a pressure to walk through the "Romans Road" or to share the exact right theological argument for faith in God, let go of that and just tell people how God has shown up in your life.

Personal experience and story are two of the most powerful means of communication. This is what you can share with others. It's the simplest, most effective way to share the gospel. When onboarding employees, share your story—including the "why" behind your work. When introducing potential clients, let them know what your business is all about. It doesn't have to be weird. In fact, the only thing that's weird is keeping such an important part of your life and your business a secret.

>

Redeemer Presbyterian Church's Center for Faith and Work conducted a survey of working believers from around the country and found that only 6 percent had shared their faith at work.[5] Six percent!

It seems that while there is plenty of conversation around faith and work, there aren't many people talking about faith *at* work. We often make this harder than it needs to be. Thankfully, the apostle Peter gives us three tips in one verse that will help us better share our faith at our jobs: "Always be prepared to give an answer to everyone who asks you to give the reason for the hope that you have. But do this with gentleness and respect" (1 Peter 3:15).

"Always Be Prepared"

Notice that Peter doesn't say always be sharing or always be talking about your faith. He just says to always be *prepared*. Sometimes sharing your faith won't fit in a sales meeting. But that doesn't mean you shouldn't be ready to talk about Jesus if the conversation allows it. Imagine if someone asked you for a recommendation of where to go to lunch. No doubt, a few restaurants come to mind that you'd gladly suggest. We can be equally prepared to draw on the life and wisdom of Jesus when those around us are asking harder questions. Find the balance between forcing a faith conversation and letting it organically occur. Always be ready, and always be praying for opportunities.

"The Hope That You Have"

What God has done in your life is not up for debate. We tend to view conversations about faith as chances to convince someone or argue someone into a relationship with God. But often that's not how it works. We can never go wrong with simply talking about what God has done in our lives. We are all broken people who need Jesus. Or, as a famous theologian once said, "Christianity is just one beggar telling another beggar where he found food." The most conversational and relatable thing we can share is why we believe and why we have hope.

"Gentleness and Respect"

Gentleness and respect are the results of healthy relationship building. People are always more receptive to information when it's coming from someone they know and trust. Which means more to you: a movie recommendation from a stranger or from a friend? It's the same with faith! Establish relationships with your employees and coworkers that are built on gentleness and respect, and let the conversations flow from there. People who have been kind to me and interested in my opinions make me want to treat them the same way. When we show the respect we'd like to receive, we open the door to be heard when talking about what matters most.

We don't need to corner our employees during their lunch breaks to share sermons with them, nor do we need to walk through an outline to salvation with every customer we encounter. But we do need to be ready to respectfully share our faith with gentleness. Paul gave Timothy the same instruction: "Preach the word; be prepared in season and out of season; correct, rebuke and encourage—with great patience and careful instruction" (2 Timothy 4:2).

I understand that this isn't always easy. But you aren't in it alone. When in doubt, you can always turn to prayer.

>

Raising funds can be every entrepreneur's greatest nightmare. It involves steady climb after steady climb to the top of Venture Capital mountain, only to walk back with your head down after each rejection. It's not easy. In fact, this is the easiest stage of the journey to become discouraged and quit.

When we first began fundraising for Bandwidth, we were striking out in every pitch meeting. Seriously. People weren't touching us with a ten-foot pole. At the time, we thought that people were prejudiced against our faith. But now I see that we were forcing our will over God's. We weren't seeking him first—we weren't seeking him at all—and instead were focused on doing what we wanted to do.

We would pray before walking into every meeting, of course. But we prayed for success. We prayed that we would walk out of those investor meetings with a certain amount of capital. But we never prayed about whether we should be raising money to begin with.

When I read Matthew 6:33 today, a specific word sticks out: "Seek *first* his kingdom and his righteousness, and all these things will be given to you as well" (emphasis added).

Faith Driven Entrepreneurs are great at seeking God, but seeking him *first* is a huge distinction. And when it comes to sharing our faith at work, when we're ministering in word, seeking God first changes the entire way we do this.

When we're praying for God to show us opportunities, to provide the right words for us to say, he will. But when we're trying to find ways to force our own evangelism strategies into conversations where they don't fit, we're being willful, not faithful.

Ministering in word doesn't stop at praying for ourselves; it means being able to pray for someone else in Jesus' name. It's seeking God first and foremost in every conversation. When someone shares a struggle or a worry with you, the first thing you can do is ask if you can take that problem to God.

Ministering in word doesn't stop at praying for ourselves; it means being able to pray for someone else in Jesus' name.

When we pray, we're communing with the living God. We're talking to God. And when we pray with somebody else present, we're inviting them into that sacred communication with God. They're now witnessing the power of God.

When you pray for someone, you're inviting them to experience God for themselves. And after you pray, you can look at someone who may have zero experience with God and say, "What I just did, you can do anytime you want. You might think I'm crazy, you might think I'm talking into the air, but I believe in a God who loves me and listens to me. And he's there for you, too."

Think about how incredibly beautiful and powerful that moment can be. Asking someone, "Is it all right if I pray for you?" is such a simple question, but it's the type of moment that God can use to open their eyes to see him.

And that's what ministering in word is all about. We're not trying to be incredible orators and apologists. We're just inviting people to see God with their own eyes. Ultimately, we're incapable of doing that for them—that's the work of the Holy Spirit.

But God is eager to use us, eager to take our words and to transform them into something truly powerful and life changing. We just have to start by opening our mouths as the Lord leads.

WANT TO SEE THIS LIVED OUT?

Visit the Faith Driven Entrepreneur website at www.faithdrivenentrepreneur.org/book-stories to watch "Beauty out of Brokenness," the story of how God brought John and Ashely Marsh through a trial that almost ended in divorce and suicide back to the work he had for them. Visit the URL to watch the full video and find thousands of other like-minded entrepreneurs going through the video study together.

CHAPTER 11

FROM EVERYWHERE TO EVERYWHERE

J. D. Greear

The day after my dad retired from the textile company where he had worked for almost forty years, his company asked him to come back to oversee the development of some new factories in East Asia. While he was there, he rubbed shoulders with Asian businessmen, the sorts of people that most missionary teams could never get close to. Because my dad is a disciple-making disciple *wherever* he goes, he was instrumental in seeing a couple of them come to faith in Christ. He even helped establish a new church there.

Later on, the local business community discovered that my mom was a professor, and they asked her if she would teach a class on English literature. Because she didn't have a background in literature, she asked, "Could I teach from the Bible instead?" To which they said, "Yes, that would be wonderful." She taught a class in which some of this region's best and brightest learned from a book they had only ever heard about.

My parents have never thought of themselves as missionaries. And yet, through entrepreneurship, they were able to advance the great commission in unprecedented ways.

At a total cost to the church of zero dollars.

As Henry mentioned earlier in this book, one of the biggest myths in the Christian church today is that the calling to use your life in God's commission is a sacred, mystical experience reserved for only a select few. More specifically, that it's a calling you can only fulfill if you're a pastor or a missionary.

But here's the truth: *all* Christians are called to ministry. Not necessarily to vocational ministry, but all Christians are called to leverage their lives for the great commission.

After all, that call was included in the initial call to follow Jesus: "'Come, follow me,' Jesus said, 'and I will send you out to fish for people'" (Matthew 4:19). When you accepted Jesus, you accepted the call to missions.

As we often say at our church, the question is no longer *if* you are called, only *where* and *how*.

This may be a new perspective for you, but historically, it's not new at all. Throughout Christian history, the greatest advances of God's mission have only rarely come from the efforts of full-time missionaries. More often than not, the gospel has been carried around the world by ordinary believers going about their business.

> **The question is no longer *if* you are called to ministry, only *where* and *how*.**

And yes, I literally mean *business*. The gospel has traveled around the world faster on the wings of business than it has even through apostolic effort. This means that your faith-driven entrepreneurship has the potential to be used by God for the great commission. God has done it countless times before. It has been his plan all along.

Consider the first Christians who spread the gospel throughout the book of Acts. As historian Stephen Neill notes in his classic book *A History of Christian Missions*,

> Few, if any, of the great Churches were really founded by apostles. Nothing is more notable than the anonymity of these early missionaries. . . . Luke does not turn aside to mention the name of a single one of those pioneers who laid the foundation. Peter and Paul may have *organized* the Church in Rome. They certainly did not found it.[6]

Dr. Neill points to the existence of three primary Christian centers by the end of the first century: Antioch, Alexandria,

FAITH DRIVEN ENTREPRENEUR

and Rome. The most remarkable thing about those centers, he says, is that we have no idea who brought the movement to them, or who planted their first churches. Just about the only detail we *do* have is that it wasn't done by pastors or missionaries.

The church at Antioch, for example, which served as *the* hub for missionary activity for the last half of the book of Acts, was planted by those scattered there after Stephen's sermon. Luke doesn't mention a single name.[7]

The same thing happened in Rome. Paul wanted to get the gospel to Rome. That journey occupies the latter half of Acts, and it was not an easy journey. To get to Rome, Paul experienced beatings, shipwrecks, snakebites, and imprisonment. But when Paul arrived, he was greeted by "brothers" (Acts 28:14, ESV).

Who were these "brothers"? Again, not apostles or missionaries or pastors. These were men whose jobs had already brought them to Rome. In other words, entrepreneurship propelled the gospel to Rome faster than traditional missionary efforts. Businessman X got there before the famed apostle Paul.

>

What if I told you that the pieces were already in place to increase the missionary force in the unreached world by 500 percent?

Currently, there are approximately forty thousand evangelical missionaries (from all denominations) living in what missiologists call the 10/40 window. (That's the area of the world located between the 10- and 40-degree latitude lines north of the equator, where the most unreached people groups live.) Every one of those forty thousand men and women are doing God's work. Praise God for it! We should pray for them. We should support them financially. We should honor their sacrifice. And we should send far more of them.

But we also need to frankly admit that forty thousand is a pretty small number when placed next to the *billions* of people who don't know Jesus.

Compare this with the roughly two million Americans working in other fields in that same 10/40 window. Half of them (that's one million) identify as Christians. Even if you skeptically write off 80 percent of those Christians as people who aren't really serious about their faith (and that really is skeptical of you!), you still have two hundred thousand Christians strategically placed among unreached people groups. That's *five times* the number of missionaries in the same region.

We hear a lot of talk today about a lack of funds in getting missionaries to tough places. But hundreds of thousands of them are already there!

Possibly, *you* are one of the ones that's there. Or, even more possibly, perhaps you are *sending* people there. Have you ever thought about your business as a potential church-planting center? I'm not saying you should transform your entire business model to suddenly become a missions organization. But if you're already sending people all throughout the world, it's worth asking why God has given you that kind of international reach.

Imagine if your Christian employees took their overseas positions with a primary identity as "disciple-making disciples," responsible to leverage whatever opportunities they have for gospel impact. Wouldn't that turn the world upside down?

Let me take it a step further. The great commission didn't originate in the United States. While Americans have more liberty than many to work abroad, we certainly aren't the only ones crossing borders with our work. In large part, Christians are already going *from* everywhere *to* everywhere. Shouldn't the great commission be going right along with them?

> **Just imagine what might happen if we *all* saw God's mission as a key part of our entrepreneurial efforts.**

Just imagine what might happen if we *all* saw God's mission as a key part of our entrepreneurial efforts. I just mentioned that if Americans shifted our thinking on this, we might effectively create two hundred thousand more missionaries on the spot. But what if Christian entrepreneurs *in every nation* began to think this way?

Suddenly two hundred thousand feels like an awfully small estimate.

>

Let me paint a picture for you of what this might look like. These are just a couple of stories I'm aware of. My guess is you can already think of several more of your own. And if you take this book seriously, we might see tens of thousands more stories just like these.

My friend Mike is head of neurology at one of our nation's most prestigious medical schools. A few times a year his university sends him to remote parts of Asia, right in the middle of some of the least-reached places on the planet. There he gives lectures to their medical professionals, consults with government workers, and mentors their medical students.

The university he serves is not a Christian one, and the places he goes are often closed to Christianity. But he said to me recently, "Because of the success God has given me, I can pretty much say whatever I want in these forums. So, as part of my teaching, I always give my testimony and explain how the gospel shapes my approach to medicine."

Mike's story reminds me of what Proverbs says: "Do you see a man skillful in his work? He will stand before kings" (22:29, ESV). If you pursue excellence in your business, at some point, even "kings" will be interested in what you have to offer.

Sometimes literally.

I know an entrepreneur in Alabama, for instance, who developed a special way of cultivating wood chips so that they soak up horse urine. As you might imagine, this kind of thing is in high demand among stable owners. And it didn't take long for some international buyers to reach out.

One of his most consistent clients now is one of the local rulers (essentially a governor) in the United Arab Emirates. He buys tons of this stuff for his horses. So now, several times a year, this Christian boy from Alabama hops on a plane to the UAE to hang out in a sultan's palace. Developing a urine-soaking wood chip got this guy where no mission board could get him.

>

Your business may not have any kind of international reach right now. Maybe you don't have international aspirations. That's fine. But hear me: *God still wants to use your business for the great commission.*

Consider that in Western culture today, more and more people have to be reached outside the church. In the United States, more than a quarter of our population says they have no religious affiliation at all. And statistics show that this group, often called the "nones," is growing.[8]

A friend of mine who pastors a church outside London pointed me to a study that indicated nearly 60 percent of British people have no plans of going to church in the upcoming year. At all. Not if a friend invites them. Not at Christmas or Easter. *Sixty percent.*

This fact, he says, radically changes how he has thought about reaching people. While the United States may not be *quite* there, we're headed that direction.

Many Christians hear stats like this and panic. I don't think that's the right response at all. God promised that his church would prevail even when confronted with gates locked by hell itself (see Matthew 16:18). In the end, *God's mission wins*. But we've got to adjust the way we think about that mission.

The future of Christianity can't be megachurches clamoring to be flashier so they can compete for pieces of a rapidly shrinking pie. We need to grow the pie. To do that, we need to reach people where they already are—in their homes, in their neighborhoods, and yes, in their businesses.

> **We need to reach people where they already are—in their homes, in their neighborhoods, and yes, in their businesses.**

God is poised to use you, entrepreneur, in that process. Don't be surprised by that: it's been his plan all along. In the book of Acts, as the gospel spread like wildfire, we read records of forty different miracles. Of those forty, thirty-nine took place outside the church. So if you're wondering where God wants to do something miraculous, chances are it's not in *my* place of employment but in *yours*.

Being in full-time ministry, I hear a lot today about a shortage of funding for missions. To be sure, the church has some work to do to fix this problem. But I wonder if God might also be at work *in* this problem. What if God is using this lack of funds as his way to remobilize Christian entrepreneurs as the tip of the gospel spear? After all, that's always been his strategy. Why wouldn't he do it today?

Why wouldn't God call us back to the book of Acts, when a bunch of merchants, carpenters, fishermen, and entrepreneurs—people without seminary degrees or formal religious training—transformed the known world for Jesus?

Entrepreneur, it's time to make yourself available to this call. Put your yes on the table before God and entrust him to use that yes for his purposes. Remember, the skills, ambitions, and dreams you have are not accidental. God gave them to you. He's got a purpose behind them.

The question isn't *if* your faith-driven entrepreneurship should be leveraged for God's mission. The only remaining question is . . . *how?*

WANT TO SEE THIS LIVED OUT?

Visit the Faith Driven Entrepreneur website at www.faithdrivenentrepreneur.org/book-stories to watch "Every Sseko Has a Story," the international story of Ben and Liz Bohannon and Sseko Designs. Visit the URL to watch the full video and find thousands of other like-minded entrepreneurs going through the video study together.

ENTREPRENEURS AND PASTORS NEED EACH OTHER

Chip Ingram

I was an entrepreneur by the time I was twelve. I regularly mowed seven or eight lawns. I had two paper routes. I loaned money to my parents at 6 percent interest.

And amid all of that, my most profitable day of the year was Halloween. I'd spend that whole night running door-to-door like a madman until my pillowcase was full of candy. Then, after storing five-cent chocolate bars in my room for a month, I'd show up to school and sell them for twenty-five cents.

So when I made the transition to become a pastor, entre-preneurship wasn't merely a curiosity; it was part of how God had designed me. I think a lot of pastors—especially church planters—can relate.

As a pastor in Silicon Valley in the 1990s, God's design couldn't have been clearer when every day I found myself drawn to the entrepreneurs who entered our doors.

Week after week, God brought Silicon Valley leaders into our church in Santa Cruz. We had venture capitalists, entrepreneurs, and business leaders whose names appeared in the news on a regular basis. And as they continued to show up, I began to realize that they had unique abilities to strengthen and empower the church in places where I found myself struggling.

I needed entrepreneurs.

We were growing at a rate well beyond what I had anticipated, so when it came to leadership paradigms, organizational structure, managing employees, assimilating new church members, balancing the budget, and other things that are normal in a business, these entrepreneurs and investors were the people I turned to for help.

As that happened, my relationship with these leaders grew deeper, and I started to realize the pain that so many entrepreneurs experience. People often look to affluent entrepreneurs and see wealth and status, but as I worked alongside them, I found every family issue you could imagine, struggles with identity, doubts about purpose, guilt about money, and so much more.

I was spending time with household names, yet I clearly remember one man in particular sharing with me that his company had just gone public, resulting in his making $100 million in a single day, but when he got home, his wife was crying. He explained that all they do is go to parties where people compare what size jets they have, and he was constantly away from his kids and felt like he had failed as a father.

People don't often see that side of entrepreneurship. Pastors especially can miss that side. Part of the reason is that many pastors tend to view successful businesspeople as financial experts or contributors rather than as sheep that need a shepherd. They're the first people we call for advice or help with fundraising. But if that's the only call they receive from us during the year, we've failed them miserably.

As much as I've needed the expertise of entrepreneurs, entrepreneurs have needed me.

So for the past twenty years, I've spent time developing relationships with the people responsible for starting and leading businesses. I've seen the dark side of entrepreneurship—the pressure, the launches, the IPOs, the crashes, the marriages that have failed, the rebellious kids, and everything in between.

For reasons I don't understand, God has given me a broken heart for high-capacity entrepreneurs. And my experience is that they are some of the most lonely, hurting, discouraged people in the world.

FAITH DRIVEN ENTREPRENEUR

These are people who have very few friends because they are so focused on guarding themselves from others who just want something from them. When everyone wants your money, your time, or your influence, it's hard to develop true relationships and friendships that aren't based on a transaction.

But pastors and entrepreneurs are alike in this. It's easy for pastors to be guarded in our relationships and to experience loneliness and burnout from the weight of our responsibilities. In fact, more than 70 percent of pastors "have no close friends they trust with personal matters," and 40 percent "have considered leaving the ministry in the last three months."[9]

I say this to point out that pastors and entrepreneurs are more alike than different. They share a lot of the same drives and the same struggles. From my vantage point, pastors and entrepreneurs share two potential flaws that, if both groups were able to lean on each other, we would be better able to notice and avoid.

Loss of Perspective

Both pastors and entrepreneurs can be addicted to growth and productivity. This makes it so easy for our identity to get mixed up with success. But when I listen to Jesus, when I think about what it means to integrate my faith with my work, I think at the heart of this problem is perspective. It all boils down to how we see.

That perspective is first upward. *How do I see God? What is God really like?* Then, it turns inward. *How do I see myself? Do I see myself? Am I asking, What did I get done and how much have I accomplished? Or am I asking, Who am I becoming?*

Lastly, our perspective turns outward. *How do I see those around me? Do I see needs around me? Do I see a platform of stewardship that I can use for others' benefit? Or do I see people to use, things to use, a platform to make others value me more?*

The upward, inward, and outward perspectives are all intertwined. The verses I turn to in order to correct my ever-wandering perspective are in Matthew 6:

> Do not store up for yourselves treasures on earth, where moths and vermin destroy, and where thieves break in and steal. But store up for yourselves treasures in heaven, where moths and vermin do not destroy, and where thieves do not break in and steal. For where your treasure is, there your heart will be also.
>
> The eye is the lamp of the body. If your eyes are healthy, your whole body will be full of light. But if your eyes are unhealthy, your whole body will be full of darkness. If then the light within you is darkness, how great is that darkness!
>
> No one can serve two masters. Either you will hate the one and love the other, or you will be

devoted to the one and despise the other. You cannot serve both God and money.

MATTHEW 6:19-24

Interestingly, Jesus says, "Do not store up for yourselves *treasures on earth*." He wants us to have treasure, but there are two treasures. He tells us not to lay up treasure on earth, because it's not a good investment. Why is earthly treasure a bad investment? Because where your treasure is, there your heart will be, and your heart isn't made for earth; it's made for heaven. The things of the earth won't satisfy us, because we've been made for God and his glory.

And then Jesus follows this with a very interesting verse. He turns straight to talking about your eye, which, candidly, feels a little off topic. But what I think Jesus is pointing out here is that our eyes inform everything. Our perspective determines our motive.

So if we're only focused inward—if we're only looking at ourselves—then what we do is going to be all about performance, performance, performance. If we only look inward, we're going to end up storing up treasure here on earth, where we are. For pastors, an inward focus often leads us to prioritize the number of people in the pews rather than the care of individual souls. For entrepreneurs, profit and self-aggrandizement can replace servant leadership and the wonderful work of creating something for the benefit of society.

But the obsession with performance fades in the light of a God who is completely satisfied with us just for who we are. The need to do more good disappears when we realize we can never be good enough, but we're saved by someone who is. We no longer have to use ourselves as the reference point for our lives. It's not about, *How hard am I working? How is the business doing? How is my work-life balance?*

Instead, our identity becomes first and foremost what God says it is—that we are dearly loved sons and daughters of infinite value because he created us, saved us, and loves us unconditionally. And that perspective informs our actions. Pastors and entrepreneurs alike face the temptation to pursue their own gain rather than to accept the free gift of grace. For two groups that are full of type-A high achievers, the need for a reminder of who God is and what he's done for us is the only thing that can keep us from losing ourselves.

Loss of Self

Dallas Willard once said that the greatest gift we ever give to anyone is never money or fame or anything that we can do for them. The greatest gift we ever give anyone is who we become.

It's all too easy for entrepreneurs to live with the ups and downs and the quarterly reports and what seed funding we have and what our percentages look like—so easy that we miss the identity formation that's happening. For pastors, caring too much about how our efforts are growing the church can lead us to ignore the way God is working through us.

But if we can, we must learn to ask, *Who am I becoming in this process? Am I becoming more loving with my wife? Would my kids say I'm a better dad because of this?* Those, of course, are much harder questions to answer and measure, but at the end of the day, they're the ones that really matter.

I recently sat around a table with some very young and successful entrepreneurs. At least four out of the seven had already done start-ups and sold them once or twice. But— I want to say this nicely—they were whining and complaining about selling early when they could have gotten a larger return than what they eventually settled for. They were all sharing similar stories of how they felt shortchanged after having sold a business for millions of dollars.

I interjected, somewhat out of the blue, and asked, "So what's the biggest challenge you're facing?" And then five of these seven guys shared major marital breakdowns they were experiencing. One guy said, "Look, this is my third start-up. My wife said that if I do this one, she'll leave me. And I'm really torn about what to do."

I was simultaneously humbled by his honesty and aghast at his values. But I think that's where the rubber meets the road. It is possible to be so wrapped up in what we are doing that we lose the things that matter most. At the end of the day, the questions we need to answer are, *What are my motives? What's my view of God? Who am I trying to impress? Who am I becoming?*

Entrepreneurs are addicted to speed and outcomes, but the life of walking with God is not a speed journey. It's one step at a time. One positive act of integrity. One God-honoring decision. Step, step, step. This process is not just a yearlong, or even decade-long, experience. The journey ends when we step through the gates of heaven.

Our lives matter far beyond the money, the companies, the employees, and all the rest. But we never seem to realize this until we look upward accurately and have people in our lives outwardly. Then we gradually come to see all that God has given us as an opportunity for stewardship. We can look to God and say, "All I know is that you have created this platform for me to be a blessing to others." And through us the life of Christ, the character of God, and the blessing of God can actually touch other people's lives and transform our own. Let me share an example of how I am still working through these competing voices in my own life.

In our ministry, Living on the Edge, we have thousands and thousands of gracious people who contribute to what God is doing. So, the other day I had a pretty good list of people who I wanted to call and say thank you to.

Over the years, I've read a lot about fundraising. The research by the professionals states that if you contact people who give, they are more likely to continue to give. And if you don't contact them, they usually won't continue to give. Pragmatically, I know it's important to call and thank our donors. But I also know that my motive is what matters to God.

The prayer I wrote in my journal was that God would help me to call these people to genuinely thank them for what they actually did for the Kingdom. I wanted to affirm the stewardship of their generosity, and not so that they'll keep on giving.

To help me keep the right focus and motive, I've developed the habit of asking them to share one thing I can pray about for them. Some share specific requests, and I pray right then and there on the phone. Others share a hurt or a challenge that begins a lengthy conversation—that's when I get to minister to them as fellow brothers or sisters in Christ, not just as donors to the ministry.

When I do this, I have to ask myself in my heart, *Am I going to call in order to receive another gift from them or in order to check this off my list? Or am I going to call with an attitude that says, "Lord, if they never give another gift, let them know I'm thankful"?*

To the people on the other end of the call, both motivations can create a similar conversation. So my motivation is entirely up to me. The same is true for all of us, pastors and entrepreneurs especially. Are we becoming the type of people who operate out of pure motives? Or are we making decisions that further our desire to serve ourselves?

Close Cousins

At the end of the day, pastors and entrepreneurs aren't that different. We're doers, we're builders, we're leaders. We want the best for the people around us. But we also want to be the best at what we do. It's not just strengths we share—our weaknesses match as well.

That's why we have to rely on each other. Because we share a lot of the same vices, temptations, and blind spots, we can walk through them together. Pastors can turn to entrepreneurs to counsel them through the struggle with performance, reminding them of God's grace. Entrepreneurs can provide an especially sympathetic ear to the pastor whose knees are buckling under the weight of leadership.

It's easy for pastors to overlook the value entrepreneurs bring to Christ's church body or to be intimidated by their success or the circles they run in. Just like it's easy for entrepreneurs to hit resistance in the church, to be frustrated by the slow pace and bureaucracy, to feel unwelcome, and to abandon the very group that wants to help them.

We want to see more happening between entrepreneurs and pastors. We want more entrepreneurs involved in the strategic visions of their local churches, helping with the business aspect of the ministries. And we want more pastors providing wisdom, guidance, and counsel to the men and women building businesses and places of influence within the community. Instead of upholding a barrier between Sunday-morning services and Monday-morning work, these two spheres can intersect with a shared faith and hope to make both groups better. Because, whether we like it or not, we need each other.

ACKNOWLEDGMENTS

No story is written by a single person . . . definitely not this one. Yes, I (Henry) have been blessed to have two coauthors on this book: Chip and J. D., two men who have helped to shape how I look at the calling of Faith Driven Entrepreneurs. But this is really a book written by many.

I want to thank first my beautiful (inside and out) wife, Kimberley. I want to thank the mother that gave birth to me and the father that has been my longest-standing fan, the one who bought me my first briefcase in college and who has invested in every one of my endeavors. Thank you, Betsey. You have exemplified selfless love, support, and encouragement while being the greatest sister a man could ever want. I want to thank my three awesome teenage boys (Benjamin, Joe, and Graham). I love you to infinity and beyond and back.

There would be no book without the three incredible men that God has placed in my path as my best friends and business partners in successive endeavors. Tom, your friendship over three decades and your faithful witness to me for a full decade before I stopped running away from God (at age twenty-eight) is a gift that I have definitely never deserved but am eternally grateful for. David, you have been the best friend and business partner a man could ever dream of having. Our adventures in business and faith have been EPIC. You have beaten me on the bike, on runs, in the pool, and down mountain slopes almost a thousand times, but I have won three or four times, and so I've got that going for me . . . which is nice. Luke, you make me so much better and allow me to have great joy while doing it. You are the best friend, business partner, and ministry partner a guy could ever want.

Justin, what a joy it has been to partner with you in Faith Driven Entrepreneur and Faith Driven Investor. You are a kindred soul and have become a good friend.

Thank you, Tim, Mark, and Daryl. Your long-standing friendship and commitment to God has inspired me and brought me great joy.

I want to thank David Wills, Todd Peterson, Todd Harper, and Jeff Johns, who have poured into my life every day for the last three and a half years as we've studied God's Word together.

Thank you, Jonny. Michael Jackson once said, "I'm a lover, not a fighter." Well, I'm a talker, not a writer (ask David, my long-suffering best friend and editor), but you have conspired with me to cover over my literary weakness, and I'm grateful.

Thank you, Jake, Michael, Jim, Kevin, David, Adora, and Tom and the entire Sovereign's Capital team for helping Luke and me achieve all that God has set out in front of us.

Thank you, Vip, Andrew, Reuben, Katherine, Megan, Sue Alice, Autumn, Morgan, Nicole, Ray, Janelle, Anna, and all that make Faith Driven Entrepreneur one of the best teams in Christendom.

Thank you, William and Rusty. I *love* cocreating with you both.

Thank you, Ford. Thank you, Kenny and Russell. Lee, we've been lifelong friends since age two. I'm very grateful for your steadfast and loyal love. Here's to another half century together!

Thank you, Mark Sears. You have shown me what a great Faith Driven Entrepreneur looks like and proven that one can also be a successful Faith Driven Investor. Now, if you only could help me to be a faith-driven athlete!

Thank you, Gabe G., Cliff D., Cliff B., Reynolds C., Michele R., Ed S., Matt R., David D., Brent B., Toby K., Chuck B., Zack M, and Casey C. It's been an honor to serve and lead with you all.

Thank you, Ted L., Todd G., Pip D., John M., Danny K., and Sean M. I'm a better man because of each of you and your friendship.

Thank you, Cam and Dave. Joe Walsh once sang, "I have accountants pay for it all." That explains about 2 percent of how you serve me. Thank you for your friendship and partnership.

I'd like to thank Dave Blanchard, Andy Crouch, Peter Greer, Brian Fikkert, Tim Macready, Chuck Welden, Tim Keller, and Andre Mann, who have shaped how I view the calling of a Faith Driven Entrepreneur.

DISCUSSION GUIDE

CHAPTER 1

1. "You're created in the image of a creative, entrepreneurial God," Henry writes (page 7). How does this inform your understanding of your work? Why do you believe you are called to be an entrepreneur?

2. Giving the example of Adam working in the Garden of Eden, the author invites us to view working as part of bearing God's image, not as a curse. In what way does this change your view of what you do?

3. "Entrepreneurship provides a place where you get to commune with God through the creative process. It provides a way through which you can love God and love others" (page 12). How have you found ways to love God and love others through your business?

CHAPTER 2

1. Henry contrasts two ways to live: out of an identity based on who we are and what we've done versus finding our identity in Christ and living for his glory. How would you describe your identity and purpose?

2. Entrepreneurs experience highs and lows, success and failure. Why does rooting your identity in Christ matter when things are going well in business and when they're not?

3. How can you bring all that you are and have to God as an entrepreneur as an act of worship? (See Romans 12:1-2.) What would that look like for you? Are there things that need to change in your business practices to make this happen?

4. Jesus calls his followers to love God and love others (see Mark 12:28-31). How are you practically living out these commandments as an entrepreneur? What are the challenges of operating a business that puts love of God and others first?

CHAPTER 3

1. Chip poses three diagnostic questions to reveal whether you view yourself as an owner or a steward: Where are you spending most of your time and energy? Where are

you spending most of your money? Whom do these efforts and expenditures benefit?

2. The "genius of generosity" brings joy to the person who understands that God owns everything and is excited about stewarding God's resources well. How can you act as a trustworthy steward of the resources God has given you as you partner with him to accomplish his purposes?

CHAPTER 4

1. "A healthy partnership founded on shared faith and shared mission can be a model for the rest of the employees, partners, vendors, and customers of what it means to work together as a team," writes Henry (pages 43–44). What examples have you seen of companies that model this kind of healthy partnership well? What makes these partnerships so effective?

2. Henry describes how great partnerships can foster transparency and vulnerability and lead to deep friendships. In your experience, what builds a culture of trust between business partners? What are the pitfalls to avoid? How important is it to have a shared faith and purpose with a business partner?

CHAPTER 5

1. J. D. warns of the dangers of making your work an idol. From the book of Ecclesiastes, he lists four areas of life in which success leads to disappointment:
   - Pleasure ultimately disappoints.
   - Even the best business wisdom sometimes fails.
   - Worldly justice systems eventually fail us.
   - The fruit of our labor crumbles.

   Which of these four do you identify with, and why?

2. In Ecclesiastes, Solomon offers four ways to find meaning in life:
   - Realize that you were created for God.
   - Arrange your life around the certainty of judgment.
   - Decide what God wants from you and pursue it.
   - Seek happiness in the present, not the future.

   Which of these truths is hardest for you to live by? Ask God to reveal your heart to you and pray about the areas he wants to change.

3. J. D. writes, "The greatest gain God can give you is not more stuff or a new challenge or a bigger platform. The greatest gain he can give you is the ability to enjoy what you have" (page 64). What might be robbing you of the ability to enjoy what you have right now?

CHAPTER 6

1. Henry and his cofounder of Bandwith, David Morken, share four values that shaped their business practices and positively affected the company culture: faith, family, work, and fitness, in that order. What can you do practically to maintain your spiritual health? Would your family members say that they know they are more important than your work? If not, what can you do to change that?

2. Colossians 3:17 says, "Whatever you do, whether in word or deed, do it all in the name of the Lord Jesus, giving thanks to God the Father through him." How does this command apply to your work? How can you invite God into the tasks you perform every day as an entrepreneur?

3. Henry tells the story of canceling a lucrative business deal because it turned out to be connected to the adult entertainment industry, which went against his core values. "When we live lives of integrity—keeping our inner principles in line with our outward actions— we are living out the calling God has placed on our lives" (page 79). What hard choices have you had to make to live out your calling as a Faith Driven Entrepreneur?

CHAPTER 7

1. "Faith Driven Entrepreneurs represent more than just themselves and their businesses—they represent the God they worship" (page 82). How does the quality of your work affect your witness as a Christian? Do you believe that doing excellent work reflects the image of God to an unbelieving world? Why or why not?

2. The author contrasts the emptiness of working hard to serve yourself with the joy of striving for excellence to serve God. When have you experienced emptiness or dissatisfaction in pursuing your own goals as an entrepreneur? When have you found joy in seeking to do great work for the glory of God?

3. How can you strive for excellence without striving for perfection? According to the author, why does this matter?

CHAPTER 8

1. "God expects us to do the impossible with what we don't have, because that paradigm means we have to trust him," Chip writes (page 93). When have you had to trust God for the impossible? What impact did that have on your faith and your life?

2. What's the difference between working *from* God's approval rather than *for* God's approval? Why is this important?

3. Chip names four things Jesus modeled that can help us move from willfulness to faithfulness: authentic humility, eternal perspective, abiding attitude, and realistic expectations (from John 13, 14, 15, and 16, respectively). Choose one of these characteristics to focus on and read the accompanying chapter in the Gospel of John. Then pray, asking God to develop that aspect of faithfulness in you.

CHAPTER 9

1. "For Christians, there's a big misconception that being an example of Christ to others means having it all together and being happy all the time," Henry writes (page 109). Do you tend to act like everything is going well when in fact you are struggling? What is one step you could take to be more honest with people in your workplace about the hard things in your life?

2. How does being honest about our brokenness invite others to come to Christ? When has someone's transparency drawn you closer to God?

CHAPTER 10

1. "The what of your business is less important than the why. And the why is so that God would be glorified in all of it" (page 118). Have you articulated the why of your business in your mission statement? What

Scriptures relate to your purpose (such as Proverbs 16:3; Matthew 6:33)? Spend some time thinking about why you do what you do, and put it in writing.

2. The author quotes 1 Peter 3:15: "Always be prepared to give an answer to everyone who asks you to give the reason for the hope that you have. But do this with gentleness and respect." How can you prepare yourself to share with others what Christ has done in your life? How can you show gentleness and respect in these conversations?

3. When someone shares a struggle or worry with you, Henry suggests asking right then, "Is it all right if I pray for you?" and praying for them in that moment. Who in your life is struggling and could use the encouragement of your prayers? Pray for that person now, and ask God for opportunities also to pray with that person.

CHAPTER 11

1. What opportunities to advance the great commission do you have as an entrepreneur that a pastor or missionary does not have? How can your faith-driven entrepreneurship be leveraged for sharing the gospel and making disciples?

2. J. D. writes, "Imagine if your Christian employees took their overseas positions with a primary identity

as 'disciple-making disciples,' responsible to leverage whatever opportunities they have for gospel impact" (page 130). Spend some time dreaming about how God could use your business for world mission and pray for God to open doors. Whom could you talk to about your dreams?

AFTERWORD

1. Pastors and entrepreneurs share a lot of the same drives and struggles, says pastor Chip Ingram. Two potential flaws he sees for both are loss of perspective and loss of self. Reflect on Matthew 6:19-24. How does this passage shape your perspective of God, yourself, and others?

2. "It is possible to be so wrapped up in what we are doing that we lose the things that matter most," Chip writes. "At the end of the day, the questions we need to answer are, *What are my motives? What's my view of God? Who am I trying to impress? Who am I am becoming?*" (pages 142–143). Prayerfully consider these questions, asking God to reveal your heart to you and bring about change as you walk with him one step at a time.

NOTES

1. Michael A. Freeman et al., "Are Entrepreneurs 'Touched with Fire'?," April 27, 2015, quoted in Henry Kaestner, Rusty Rueff, and William Norvell, "The Entrepreneur's Hidden Battle with Depression with Max Anderson," September 24, 2019, episode 75, in *Faith Driven Entrepreneur*, podcast, 38:32, https://www.faithdrivenentrepreneur.org/podcast-inventory/2019/9/24/episode-75-max-anderson-depression-among-entrepreneurs.
2. Blaise Pascal, *Pensées*, number 172, emphasis added.
3. Ron Friedman, "Regular Exercise Is Part of Your Job," *Harvard Business Review*, October 3, 2014, https://hbr.org/2014/10/regular-exercise-is-part-of-your-job.
4. Madeleine L'Engle, *Walking on Water* (New York: Convergent, 2016), 113.
5. Timothy Keller and Katherine Leary Alsdorf, *Every Good Endeavor: Connecting Your Work to God's Work* (New York: Penguin, 2012), 258.
6. Stephen Neill, *A History of Christian Missions*, 2nd ed., edited by Owen Chadwick (Harmondsworth, Middlesex, England: Penguin Books, 1990), 22.
7. See Acts 11:19-21.
8. Pew Research Center, "In U.S., Decline of Christianity Continues at Rapid Pace," October 17, 2019, https://www.pewforum.org/2019/10/17/in-u-s-decline-of-christianity-continues-at-rapid-pace/.
9. "Seventy Percent of Pastors Are Lonely," Stand Strong Ministries, accessed February 2, 2021, https://www.standstrongministries.org/articles/seventy-percent-of-pastors-are-lonely/#:~:text=Research%20shows%20that%2040%25%20of,they%20first%20joined%20the%20ministry.

ABOUT THE AUTHORS

HENRY KAESTNER cofounded the Faith Driven Entrepreneur and Faith Driven Investor ministries, and has been a catalyst behind both movements. He and his team seek to serve faith-driven investors, funds, partners, advisors, and entrepreneurs through content and community. Recently, they launched a platform called Marketplace, where Christian investors are connected to faith-driven funds and direct deals, and where Christian entrepreneurs can source capital at market and concessionary returns as appropriate.

Henry is also a cofounder and partner at Sovereign's Capital, a private equity and venture capital management company that invests in faith-driven entrepreneurs in Southeast Asia and the United States from its offices in Silicon Valley; Washington, DC; and Jakarta, Indonesia. Prior to cofounding Sovereign's Capital, Henry was cofounder, CEO, and then chairman of Bandwidth (NASDAQ: BAND) and its sister company, Republic Wireless (which spun out of Bandwidth in 2016). Together, those companies have grown from $0 to more than $400 million in revenue. The founding values of Bandwidth are faith, family, work, and fitness (in that order). Prior to cofounding Bandwidth with David Morken, Henry founded Chapel Hill Brokers (a predecessor to ICAP Energy), an institutional energy derivatives broker that became the top-ranked electricity broker in the country.

Henry has been involved in a number of other ministries and philanthropic activities. He cofounded DurhamCares, was a founding board member of Praxis, and sits on a variety of business and ministry boards, including Valley Christian Schools, where his three boys attend. Go Warriors!

Henry is a member of the broader church in the Bay Area, attends Venture Christian Church in Los Gatos, California, and serves as an elder in the Presbyterian Church in America. Henry lives in Los Gatos with his wife, Kimberley, and their three sons.

J. D. GREEAR is the pastor of The Summit Church in Raleigh-Durham, North Carolina. Under Pastor J. D.'s leadership, The Summit has grown from a plateaued church of three hundred to one of over ten thousand, making it one of Outreach magazine's "top 25 fastest-growing churches in America" for many years running.

Pastor J. D. has led The Summit in a bold vision to plant

one thousand new churches by the year 2050. In the last fifteen years, the church has sent out more than one thousand people to live on church-planting teams—in North Carolina, across the United States, and around the world.

Pastor J. D. completed his PhD in theology at Southeastern Baptist Theological Seminary and served in Southeast Asia with the International Mission Board. He is currently serving as the sixty-second president of the Southern Baptist Convention. He and his wife, Veronica, live in Raleigh, where they are raising their four children.

CHIP INGRAM is the teaching pastor and CEO of Living on the Edge, an international teaching and discipleship ministry. Chip's direct, practical teaching style helps everyday believers apply God's truth to relevant issues, relationships, and challenges. Reaching more than a million people each week, his teaching can be heard online and through hundreds of radio and television outlets worldwide. In his winsome, down-to-earth way, he reveals biblical truth about God's perspective on marriage, understanding love and sex, raising kids, money, and how to live the Christian life in today's culture. A pastor for over thirty years, Chip is the author of many books, including *Culture Shock*; *The Real Heaven*; *The Real God*; *The Invisible War*; and *Love, Sex, and Lasting Relationships*.

Chip and his wife, Theresa, have four grown children and twelve grandchildren and live in California.

FAITH DRIVEN
—ENTREPRENEUR—

Entrepreneurship is a lonely journey...
But it doesn't have to be.

Join a small group of 10 other entrepreneurs meeting weekly and wrestling
through what it means to be a Faith Driven Entrepreneur.

Don't Go It Alone

The entrepreneurial journey is often a lonely one. But it doesn't
have to be that way. Faith Driven Entrepreneur has designed an
eight-week video study that you can walk through with a community of entrepreneurs.

Together, we'll watch videos that feature teaching from Henry
Kaestner and J. D. Greear—as well as real-life stories of entrepreneurs living these lessons out—and discuss them as a group. These
small groups are for aspiring entrepreneurs, those looking for advice, or anyone wanting to connect with a like-minded community.

Join a group at faithdrivenentrepreneur.org/watch-with-a-group.

FAITH DRIVEN
—ENTREPRENEUR—

Faith Driven Entrepreneur Live

Think of the one-day virtual conference as a family reunion for the movement streaming to 100+ Watch Parties across the globe to hear from others on the journey and be reminded that **you are not alone**.

Find Your Place

Faith Driven Entrepreneur hosts regular events that give you a chance to connect with other entrepreneurs, learn from those who have been in your shoes, and grow from the counsel and wisdom of others who have experienced every form of success (and failure) you can imagine.

Whether you want to participate in our monthly gatherings or the annual conference, there's a place for you. No matter what phase of the journey you're on, you can find somewhere to meet, connect, grow, and learn.

Find out more at faithdrivenentrepreneur.org/community.

FAITH DRIVEN
—ENTREPRENEUR—

Find Faith Driven Investors

Are you a Faith Driven Entrepreneur looking for philanthropic or investment capital? Marketplace is where faith capital collides with faith-driven deals. It's where every investment has an impact.

Some of the leading family offices, accredited investors, and private equity groups of the Faith Driven Movement use Marketplace. With your account, you get a chance to feature your deck, profile, and company history in front of active investors looking to put capital to work. Whether you're looking for investment capital, seeking help with your pitch, or desiring monthly coaching sessions with other leaders, Marketplace is right for you.

Apply to have your deal featured at faithdrivenentrepreneur.org /marketplace.